I'M STILL LIVING
by Chava Kwinta

I'M STILL LIVING
by Chava Kwinta

Simon & Pierre Publishing Company Limited
Toronto, Ontario, Canada

Copyright © 1974 by Chava Kwinta.
All rights reserved.

No part of this book may be reproduced or transmitted in any form by any means, electronic or mechanical, including photocopying and recording, information storage and retrieval systems without permission in writing from the publisher, except by a reviewer who may quote brief passages in a review.

Published simultaneously in the United States by Books Canada Inc., 33 East Tupper Street, Buffalo, N.Y. 14203.

ISBN 0-88924-035-3(hardcover)/ISBN 0-88924-053-1(paper)
   2 3 4 5/79 78 77 76

Simon & Pierre Publishing Company Limited
Order Department
P.O. Box 280 Adelaide Street Postal Station
Toronto, Ontario, Canada M5C 2J4

Printed and bound in Canada by The Hunter Rose Company.
Staff Writer, Madeline Thompson
Designer, Catherine P. Wilson
Typographers, Dari Haddon and Robert Tracy
Cover Artist, Ma Shiu Yu

This book has been published with the help of friends. It is hoped that the positive values of the human spirit shown in this book will serve as an example to all.

Marian M. Wilson
Publisher

I acknowledge the assistance of Shoshana Perla for the translation of my work from Hebrew to English. I also acknowledge the assistance of Haim Gluckstein who translated my Foreword from Hebrew to English, and who translated certain paragraphs from Hebrew to English.

I thank David and Jocelyn Harvey for their assistance.

C.K.

"Il y a quelque chose d'humiliant à être homme et ne pas lutter contre le malheur."

"There is something humiliating about being a man and not fighting against suffering."
       Alexandre Chenevert (The Cashier)
          by Gabrielle Roy

Preface

The horrors of the holocaust have been written about many times, but the story has to be told again and again. It has to be repeated time and time again so that those who are aware will be reminded, and those who are too young to remember will begin to know and understand.

Chava Kwinta was born in Sosnowiec, a town very representative of the industrial part of Poland. There was the old town in the centre with century-old houses, and little suburbs where life went on with little excitement but much decency, with maybe little glamour but a lot of reliability.

The life standard was somewhat higher in the suburbs and the problems of day-to-day living were not of any great enormity.

And then there was the other part of the town which housed those who made Sosnowiec a prosperous town, though not for themselves.

Sosnowiec is a mining town and the miners lived and worked as miners live and work everywhere. The working hours are spent in darkness under the ground, and the few hours above are often misspent.

This then is the background of a girl who lived in her own suburban surroundings and who went to a school where her classmates were mostly from the other side of the borderline. It is told simply and beautifully; it is told honestly and without any attempt at sensationalism or dogmatic preaching which is so often seen in this kind of autobiography.

Chava Kwinta is an unusual person. After the years that she spent under indescribable circumstances, she still managed to return to the world as a complete human being.

Her story, "I'm Still Living", ends in Sweden where the few children who were saved—either by intention or coincidence—were moved to create or re-create some kind of assemblage of sanity. That was a first attempt to place her in an environment suitable to compensate her for the years she had lost.

She had the opportunity to go to a school and this school created an atmosphere which attempted to make up for the past. The language was Jewish and Polish and the teachers were understanding. The focus was not to learn the three R's but rather to re-establish the pride in being a part of a culture that proudly existed for thousands of years.

It had its effect on her. She felt safe enough with her newly regained confidence to do what she always felt should be done. She wanted to go to "The Place" where the Jew is not a minority. She wanted to go to the land which had been beckoning for two thousand years.

It was a great disappointment that she missed the classical ship, the "Exodus".

After several frustrating months in France, she was finally granted all the necessary papers required in order to emigrate to Australia and given a proviso to make a stopover in Israel.

The ship docked in Haifa. There was no doubt then nor had there ever been any question in her mind whether to remain there or continue her journey.

She had finally found the land—the land she dreamt about as a child, when she would ask her grandfather, "Why don't we leave if they don't want us here? Why don't we go home?"

Chava wanted to be a soldier, as young people do, to defend what they believe in. At that time there were not enough guns to give out to the girls. So she did what a woman would do—she took care of the wounded. The Hadassah Hospital in Tel Aviv was the recipient of those who were wounded and was the place where helping hands were needed.

Gradually from an unqualified girl who did what she had to do she became a qualified nurse. She learned the language which was hers by birth and not by knowledge. When she graduated as a nurse in Tel Aviv it was in the Hebrew language.

One day a wounded man was brought to the hospital ward—a man who fought for what he believed in. She took care of him and he is now her husband.

Her love and concern for her people led her to spend her spare hours studying at the University of Tel Aviv the background of the Jews and the Jewish contribution to the history of the world.

After fifteen years in Israel, she and her family moved to Canada. She wanted to be close to her father who had emigrated to Detroit and she wanted to be close to her husband's family who was Canadian.

Chava Kwinta lives in Toronto with her husband and three daughters.

When she came to this country, she not only mastered the English language but succeeded in becoming a registered nurse in Canada completing a special course in cardio-vascular disease at the University of Toronto qualifying her to be a part of the famous "heart unit".

When asked why she had left the promised land, she answered, "In the years I was there, I contributed. In need, I will always be in the right place at the right time."

Her main aim is to teach children their heritage and keep awake the awareness of their past. She will very soon hold a certificate to teach Jewish cultural history at a high school level in separate schools.

The validity of her writing is that even as a young girl, she could see what great philosophers took a lifetime to see—that the world, even under its most bleak circumstances, is not black and white but shades of grey in its full spectrum. There were good Jews and bad Jews, good Poles and bad Poles, and, yes, there were bad Germans and there were some good Germans too. Again there is no hatred within her writing, only the naively factual report of one who is a 'survivor'.

It is not a question of who is to blame directly or indirectly—the point is that the killing must be stopped.

Perhaps this book will contribute to this philosophy.

Rolf Kalman, General Editor

Foreword

"Wake up, darling—get up, love! We're free! Can you hear what I'm saying? We're free!" The words filtered through a haze. "I won't let you die now, you've got to live, do you hear, Chava'le?" Now the voice began to plead, "Oh please, please open your eyes. Look around and see how our dream has come true. We've been saved! The British army has liberated our camp. No more Nazis . . . ."

Was it my sister speaking or my aunt? Did I hear clearly? I don't know. For three days I was half-conscious. Sometimes I would open my eyes for a moment and then fall back to sleep again. Once I murmured, "A sip of tea," and by some miracle my request was filled at once! Again and again I was given the lovely hot tea, sweetened with real sugar. It exerted a magical effect and before long I was opening my eyes more frequently. The improvement in my condition awakened the hopes of my aunt and my sister as they sat on the floor beside me. Every time I regained consciousness for a few minutes, they tried to tell me the good news, but I was too weak to grasp the meaning of their words. I was still in a haze, falling back to sleep, sweating, exhausted from the months of starvation and fear. It was not until the third day following the arrival of the British troops and the liberation of Bergen-Belsen on April 15, 1945, that I opened my eyes wide and sat up.

All that was happening around me did not immediately pene-

trate my mind. I sat looking at the uncommon activity in our block, with soldiers—both men and women—coming and going, endlessly snapping our pictures. Suddenly I noticed that all around me the women and girls were eating foods we had not seen for many months, things we had almost forgotten the taste and form of. And all of the girls looked so happy, it seemed, moving freely in and out without any restriction or caution or fear. Everything was like a dream, and I really thought this is a dream, for it was exactly as for years I had dreamed it would be. Yet every passing moment brought new revelations.

Very cautiously, I asked my aunt and sister where all that delicious hot sweet tea was coming from. In the course of the war the habit of keeping silent had grown strong; superfluous questions were forbidden. Even now, I asked my question as discreetly as possible. Then my aunt and sister explained that while I lay sick and unknowing, we had been liberated, that I was no longer only a number doomed to die in a Nazi gas chamber, a prisoner without the right to life. Germany had been defeated. Once again I was an ordinary girl. True, I was different from other girls of my age, very different in many ways, but—I was free!

I simply could not believe my own aunt and sister. The whole thing looked too preposterous to me.

But gradually my mind began to grasp the fact that overnight all our lives had changed. Excited at last, I tried to rise and see with my own eyes the changes that had taken place, as if to prove to myself that what they had been telling me was really true. Several times I tried to stand up but I was incapable of taking a single step. A frail little "musselman"—a living cadaver—dizziness made my head whirl. Lying down on the floor again, I resigned myself to waiting another day in the hope of becoming a bit stronger.

Meanwhile the stream of visitors never ceased. Because we were so young, my sister and I drew the attention of all who came. They were already accustomed to mature musselmen, but here were child-musselmen, a specimen they were seeing for the first time, and so we were photographed again and again. They wondered how we came to be here at all, for according to Hitler's "Final Solution", Jewish children were doomed from the start. The enormous attention my sister and I were receiving made me uncomfortable. Why did they all stop to stare at me? Was my appearance so frightful? Don't I look human at all anymore, I thought? I had no mirror and could not see that I was literally skin and bones and wore that peculiar look of suspicion and terror. Every movement, every noise, and especially the sight of a man in uniform, made me shudder. I knew that I was among friends, people who had come to help and rescue us, but I could not control my instinctive panic. Weak and frightened, I sat down on the floor, wrapped myself up in a black blanket, and waited.

Toward evening on the third day of our liberation, representatives of the Red Cross entered our block and made the rounds of the sick. They wanted to take me to the hospital, but I resisted, shouting and crying, "I don't want to go!" Under the Nazis, going to the hospital meant death. So ferociously did I scream that the Red Cross people somehow understood and left me in peace. But through their intervention, I was thereafter given special meals high in protein and vitamins several times a day.

As my body grew stronger, my spiritual strength increased too. After a few days I stood up and felt I could walk about without help. I left our barrack to wander along the block and met a young blond soldier with light blue eyes. I looked at him in wonder and thought to myself, he must be a hero, superhuman. Surrounded by skeleton-like musselmen for so long I had quite forgotten how a normal, healthy young man looked. For the first time since our liberation I felt suddenly happy. My appearance must have touched the young soldier, for he asked in broken German, "What is your name, little girl? How old are you? Where are you from?" I could not answer him. Thinking I did not understand he tried to improve his German and asked again, but still I could not speak.

At that moment I simply could not talk about myself. Only now, more than twenty years after my meeting with the British soldier, can I begin to relive this period of my life. Now I am impelled to tell my story, particularly for the young people born in the generation after mine.

To you this book is dedicated. There is so much I have to tell you.

One special, to me, sacred purpose motivates me—to explain to the young Jewish people of today why we did not rebel en masse: what were the reasons and the circumstances, what mistakes were committed, how they may be avoided in the future, and who were the guilty ones who could have helped and yet did not. The chapter we represent in the annals of the Jewish people might well have been written differently; what was the reason for our seeming indifference toward our fate? This too shall be dealt with, as well as the fact that you young people have no cause to feel ashamed of the generation that brought you into the world. You deserve to know the truth, to learn it from a person who lived through this period from start to finish and knew from personal experience the realities of the situation as they were perceived by a child of the time.

Chapter One

"Life is so beautiful"—you can hear this platitude almost everywhere. Poets through the ages have sung its praises, comparing it to blossoming flowers, to sunrise, and light. The beauty of life begins with childhood. Did I enjoy childhood at all? Did another million children who suffered my fate have any childhood? The problems I was forced to solve, the endless battle I had to wage for mere existence, transformed the child I was into a mature person who had to think and behave with a grown woman's sense of responsibility, to be extraordinarily alert to everything going on around me, to lie awake at night trying to think of solutions. I was young in years but terribly old mentally and emotionally. In this respect I was not an exception. Under the pressures of persecution and war the instincts of little tots develop at a dizzying speed and children mature long before their time.

But as a young girl I loved my birthplace, a town called Sosnowiec, in Poland. I was attached to every little corner in it, to the house in which I lived, the sand I played in, the yard where I played hide-and-seek with other children. We, my sister, parents and I, lived in a suburb of the town, in an apartment building on the main street owned by my grandfather. The building housed a number of families including my grandparents and my aunts, three of my mother's sisters. It was not a rich community, mostly miners, factory workers and shopkeepers (my father had a small shop); we were a mixture of Jews and Polish Catholics and all the children played together in and around the many apartment buildings. There were a few private *houses on the side streets but we were, in total, a community of working class people, intent on making a living. I remember looking into the street early in the morning, watching the coalminers on their way to the coal fields or returning from the night shift, very tired, their lanterns, sometimes still lit, swinging in their hands. They had the hardest struggle of all to keep themselves going. They were poor, ill-educated and had little hope of a better future for themselves or their children, and their pay-day drunk sprees on the first of every month were a regular part of our community landscape. I would watch from our apartment, for one did not venture into the streets on these nights, and puzzle over their escapades and violence. We had wine in the house for the Sabbath but drunken bouts were not part of our Jewish family life. Still, they were part of my childhood memories, as familiar as the rest of my neighbourhood. But, as I grew to consciousness, I often felt strange there for the children who were my playmates in our building's courtyard and on the street sometimes treated us as if we did not belong. They were in the habit of suddenly calling out "dirty Jews" and shouting "Jew kids, go to Palestine!" Then we would be pushed and shoved. We felt debased and confused. What did it mean, "Jew kids, go to Palestine"? Was it an insult or an honor? Finally, we decided to ask Mother. "These are uneducated children, they don't know any better," she said. "If they make any trouble, you just keep away from them." But sometimes it was hard to find a well-educated child!*

When those moments occurred, our innermost souls were wounded, for we not only heard insults from our friends but were forced to hold our tongues. Whenever I grew angry or rebellious, I was told not to "start anything". "You just keep away from them." This conditioning, given to so many Jewish children in Europe, affected their behaviour and had a far-reaching effect as events ran their course with the coming of the Nazis.

Chapter Two

"Darling," said Grandmother, "you will soon be seven years old and I am preparing a surprise for you. Since your birthday isn't until November I'm giving you the regular schoolbag all grandchildren get when entering first grade now." This traditional prize elated me, for I had been waiting impatiently to start school. Like any other child, I was terribly excited when mother decided to celebrate the occasion with a big family gathering and promised I could invite all my girl-friends. I felt very important. I kept asking mother whether I might include this friend and that one, and together we planned the party. I began to count the days. Time seemed to pass unbelievably slowly, but sooner or later, just as everything arrives, so did the day I so much looked forward to. I was happy, how happy, in family and with my lot. I loved my people and they loved me, my small and cosy world was whole and complete. It was only when I left our house that I felt some vague, imponderable hostility, as if oxygen were lacking in the air, but at seven I thought that this was the way things had to be, and at home I tried to shut out the things that disturbed me.

Our parents, the adults, understood this feeling of alienation we faced everyday in the outside world and they liked to group together, if they could, to give their children a sense of security, a feeling of belonging. In many areas of Poland there were whole communities of Jews, self-sufficient, with their own schools and community services. But where I lived, although we had many relatives around us, it was difficult to separate ourselves from the general public and impossible to isolate us as far as school was concerned. My parents therefore enrolled me in the first grade of the general elementary school. There were twenty-eight of us in the class. The Jewish pupils were three girls and one boy. On the first day of school I got dressed up in my best Saturday clothes and, equipped with my brand new schoolbag, went proudly on my way. When the bell rang in the school yard we formed a line and went into our room. Each child was assigned a specific seat. After introducing herself, our teacher announced: "Children, every morning we will begin our lesson with a prayer, like real Christians." She made no mention of the fact that other faiths exist but directed us all to rise and recite in unison the prayer she named. We four were the only ones who remained silent. One after another of the children looked at us in surprise, and during recess I was repeatedly asked the same question: "Why didn't you pray? You stood there and didn't open your mouth." "I am a Jew," I replied.

These children, of course, returned home that day eager to tell their families everything that had happened at school, and they didn't forget to mention the strange children who said they were "Jews" and didn't say the prayer. Nearly all of them were given the same explanation: "Jews hate Jesus and the Christians; they killed Our Lord." We quickly felt the effects of this explanation. Little children of seven, accepting unquestioningly the word of their parents, couldn't distinguish between myth and fact, truth and fantasy. They acquired a feeling of hostility toward us and instinctively dissociated themselves from the four of us. Every now and then one would ask me whether we had been among those who crucified Christ. "I don't know what you're talking about," I would say. "I've never hurt anyone." Once I asked my mother whether anyone in our family had ever killed a man: "Did you? Did Father? Or Grandpa?

Or Grandma?"

"No, my child," Mother replied, startled. "Why do you ask such a thing?" "Because the children at school accuse us of killing Jesus. Is that true?"

Mother did not laugh. "No," she said. "You are too young now to understand these false accusations. When you grow up, you'll understand what terrible harm they can cause."

In the days that followed we accustomed ourselves to the daily routine of school work. During recess the children would form a circle and sing and dance. Whenever I tried to join, they would not let me in. Thus repulsed, I looked around for my Jewish friends and they welcomed me warmly. I had friends who wanted my company. I was pleased. From the start I took this arrangement for granted; this was the way things were: we are different and they are different, and that's that. I knew no other way. I was happy to be at school and to have the chance to study everything I wanted to know. Every day at recess the four of us fell into the habit of standing off to the side, eating our sandwiches and watching our classmates playing. But we changed our place daily, rotating the corners at which we stood.

After a day of study under strict discipline, when the more energetic boys found it hard to sit quietly in their seats and concentrate on the lesson, the ringing of the closing bell signaled the release of all their mischievousness. Once outside they ran and jumped and shouted. Their favourite trick was to throw stones at their schoolmates, then hide or run away. If a child was hit and the culprit identified, the victim's family immediately complained to the other boy's parents, who spanked their son soundly. But if it was only one of us Jewish children who was hurt and our parents complained, the boy was merely *scolded. In no time at all the mischief-makers recognized which victims were open to their attacks. In our school more than one Jewish pupil came home with a bloody head—in the summer from a stone, in the winter from a hard snowball. Yet all our parents reacted in the same way: we were not to fight with them, not to throw rocks or snowballs back at them, but to try to avoid them, to go home by a roundabout way if need be. For if, God forbid, one of our Jewish boys were to hit and injure one of theirs, he might bring disaster on his whole family. This submissive attitude was imbued in us from a very early age, before we could ask "why and whatfore". "We know better; we are older and more experienced. Listen to what we tell you." And, of course, at that age we listened and obeyed.*

Weeks passed. Winter was approaching. Silvery white snow began to cover all the roof tops. Everything looked different. The leaves had fallen and the bare trees were shrouded in gleaming snow, a sure sign that the holidays were coming. A week before school closed, when the class was quite noisy, the teacher asked for silence because she had a very pleasant announcement to make. The room became still at once; one could hear the buzzing of a fly. "Children," the teacher said, "if you promise to be good the whole year through, St. Nicholas will come to visit our room and distribute presents to everybody." A delighted shout greeted this announcement and we all went home with the wonderful news. I burst into the house and before even saying hello to my mother I told her St. Nicholas was coming to school with gifts for everybody. Mother did not say a word, but that night I could hardly sleep from excitement and worry about how he could squeeze his sack of presents and his full figure through the narrow chimney of the school. All night I dreamed of a white-bearded man wearing a red hat handing out toys and sweets; I myself received a large box tied with a beautiful red ribbon . . . .

On the glad day our entire class came dressed in holiday clothes and in a very festive mood. We all tried to guess what St. Nicholas would bring us. I could not decide what I wanted most. Whatever it was I wanted it to be a big surprise. Tense, I sat among the others waiting for the happy moment. Then the door opened and in he came, with his sack full of boxes.

"Good morning, sweet children," he said merrily. "I've decided to bring presents for all of you if you promise to be good throughout the year and to do what your teacher asks." "We promise! We promise!" a chorus of voices answered impatiently. The tension was great as our names were called out and each child in turn came up to receive a nicely wrapped package of sweets. My heart was pounding and I kept hoping the next name called would be mine. But all my excitement was in vain. All the children received presents except for the four of us. We were outside the happy circle. Two of my girl-friends wept all the way home. The boy and I did not cry but walked in sad silence. We were all thinking the same question: WHY? Why are we always left out? In what way are we different from everyone else? And we hurried home to ask our mothers.

When I reached home my face was very pale and my sadness was immediately apparent to my mother, who asked me at once what had happened. Her response was quick and soothing: I had no reason to be sad because I had not received a gift at school, for to children St. Nicholas especially liked he paid a personal visit during the night, leaving a present under the child's pillow. I had only to wait until morning . . . When I awoke there was indeed a beautiful box of candy under my pillow. Not for a moment did I doubt that it had come from St. Nicholas, who liked me so much he took additional pains for my sake.

Chapter Three

The first year in school was over. I had learned to read fluently and excelled in the other subjects as well. Books were a revelation for me, and I especially loved the tales by the Grimm brothers and stories about old, wise men who "know everything". As I read book after book, I came to the conclusion that the wisdom of old people often helped to untangle the most complicated situations and to find a happy solution to every problem.

As a natural consequence I began to ply my own grandfather with endless questions. The narrow boundaries I felt limiting my daily life weighed heavily on me and awakened in me questions for which I could not find answers. One day Grandpa asked me, "How was it at school today? Do you make any good?" "Yes, Grandpa," I replied. "I'm learning everything fine, but do you know, the children call me 'dirty Jew' and things like that and keep saying 'go to Palestine'! So why don't we really move away to some other city? Could we do that, Grandpa?"

"Darling," said Grandpa with a sad smile, "this won't solve the problem. It's the same everywhere. Everywhere we are harassed. We shall be everywhere Jews."

"Then why don't we go to live in a different country? Is it the same all over the world?"

His face became very grave. He hesitated a moment and then said, "I don't know, darling; I cannot answer your question."

This was a bit of a shock to me. I thought old people knew all the answers to all the questions. Still I persisted. "Grandpa, who do those letters you receive come from? Do you have brothers or sisters somewhere?"

"Yes, dear," he nodded, "I have two brothers in America. They live in a city named Cincinnati."

"Then why don't we go to America too? Do they persecute Jewish children in the schools in Cincinnati? In Cincinnati do they attack old Jews in the street, and throw stones and break windowpanes?"

"No, child, I don't think they have these troubles there; at least my brothers don't write to me about such things. They are happy, got nice jobs, their children learn, and I am happy to know they are getting along well." He drew a deep breath as if remembering the details of what happened many years before. "Actually, after my older brother went with his family to America, he sent me an affidavit and a ticket to bring me over there, for we were very close to each other, but I let my younger brother go instead. You see, he was poor while I was a successful businessman. I had a big house, a business of my own. I had many friends and met them in the synagogue every day. I was attached to all this. These were my life, so why would I rush off to America or any other place?"

As he paused I asked, "Grandpa, were Jews not mistreated at that time?"

"Yes, but not like now," he answered. "We were used to it and *we tried to keep our distance and not annoy them. We kept things quiet in our part of town and—the main thing, we tried to live according to tradition and the Law. When I put on my Sabbath clothes on Friday evening and go to the synagogue, I feel as if Providence watches over my home. Everything looks so beautiful and I don't see anything that goes on outside. So it is with all our holidays and festivals. Will I ever feel like that anywhere else?"*

I was too young to appreciate his way of looking at things or to understand exactly why his replies seemed so inadequate. "Grandpa, isn't there any place in the world where we wouldn't have to be afraid, the way my Polish girl-friends are not afraid?"

He thought it over and then replied, "Truth to tell I never thought about that. Do you know what we have to do, dear?" "What?" I said eagerly, as if a real revelation were coming at last. "To pray," he said. "To be pious and believe in God and He will help us. The trouble is that there are too many sinners in our world and because of them the good people also suffer." Then he asked when would I start going to Hebrew school to learn Torah and prayers. "Soon," I replied and left the house, disappointment filling my heart.

From this conversation on, all the urges I had felt toward opposing injustice gradually faded away. In those years every solution my eager youth conceived was shrugged off as impractical or ineffective. The only hope adults offered was prayer, observing the laws of the Torah and performing good deeds—God would return His people to Palestine in His own time. In order that I might hasten my people's redemption I was sent to "heder"—school to learn to read Hebrew and to pray. The teacher was a man who gave us lessons in a room in his apartment, one hour four times a week. My lesson was set for six o'clock. Preceding our group was a class of boys twelve to fourteen years of age. I always came a little early and invariably I found the same boy—his name was Shmuel—standing by the door. Shmuel, who was about thirteen, was a handsome boy with large, clever black eyes. He impressed me as unusually bright, and I could not understand why he seemed so undistressed by being expelled from the classroom every day. How could he be so disobedient, I wondered to myself? Did he not care to study religion and the Torah? Was it not his duty to follow the ways of his forefathers? Did he not know our troubles must be solved through prayer? I remembered what Grandpa had told me, of course. At this age I was too shy with boys to ask Shmuel these questions, though every day before Hebrew class I practised them. Each time I set out for class I wondered, would Shmuel be cast out in the hall again today?

As our lesson began, the teacher was always a little nervous because of Shmuel, but he gradually relaxed because we girls were much more quiet and attentive than the boys who preceded us. Every time I returned home I told my mother about Shmuel, and once she called him a troublemaker. But he was part of the picture I formed of the teacher's waiting room, and I was always glad to see him.

Then one day I opened the door and could not find Shmuel. I was happy to think he had changed his ways and started to behave in class. But this was not the case. After several minutes had passed the teacher opened the door and invited us to enter the room. The lesson would begin a little late, he said, because of a discussion he was having with Shmuel. I wondered whether the teacher had decided Shmuel would not respond to being sent from the room and was trying a new technique, or whether Shmuel had decided to placate the teacher by discussing his problems with him. But it soon became clear that neither of *these was the reason. Shmuel was highly intelligent and had reached an age at which injustice distressed him. He could not reconcile himself to what he saw all about him, and his disturbances in class were only his way of drawing the teacher's attention and trying to provoke a meaningful discussion. He had at last succeeded.*

The discussion began with Shmuel's earnest declaration that he had nothing personal against the teacher or the subjects he was teaching. On the contrary, he thought the teacher very competent. He was a man who took a lively interest in many fields and was active in the Zionist movement, and for this reason Shmuel wished to ask him a number of questions.

"I believe," Shmuel said, "that you do not fulfill your duty as a teacher by teaching us alone; you ought to gather our parents together and teach them as well. Their way of life is wrong. Do you really think they are right in sending their children to learn Torah when all the time at home they teach their children to be slaves? Every Jewish boy and girl is taught the same thing by his parents, to submit to every insult at school and not rebel. I don't agree to that. If sometimes I fight back and my mother hears about it, she becomes pale and shivers: I ask her why and always she says, 'You know we are Jews. If you hurt a Christian boy you will bring disaster on our family and the community.' I thought it over the first time she said this and I could not sleep all night. The next day I borrowed a book on religion from the library. I found out that there are many faiths that people practise. There are Catholics, Protestants, Moslems, Buddhists, Jews and others. But only we are being persecuted everywhere. Is there something wrong in our faith? If so, I don't want to learn it! That's why I disturbed you in class."

The teacher thought for a long while and then answered slowly, without any feeling of hostility or aggression. "Our people have a long history and a rich and varied culture. We have nothing to be ashamed of. We always fought against our oppressors in ancient times. We have a rich literature. Our Bible was, and still is, a moral influence for the whole world."

"So why did our parents forget their real origin? Why are they afraid of every hoodlum and drunkard?" Shmuel asked.

"Do you all think Shmuel is right?" asked our teacher. "Yes!" we shouted in unison. And one student added, "That's exactly how we all feel, but we didn't dare to say so."

"Very well," answered our teacher. "It is late now to begin, but I suggest we start discussing these problems tomorrow. Now you must go home for your families will be worrying about you. Good night, children."

All the way home I went over and over in my mind every word that had been spoken. I swore never to miss one of these discussions. When my family asked, "How was it today in Hebrew class?" I answered, "All right," but I avoided telling them how it really was.

Next day I came very early and sat waiting for the teacher to speak. It was obvious he was excited and pleased. Slowly he began, "You see, children, we are not just a religious sect. We are a nation, and a nation needs a state. Two thousand years ago we had our state, we were no different from any other nation, but now...."

Here he launched into an animated lecture on the history of the Jewish people and its state, the destruction of the holy Temple in Jerusalem in the year 70, the suffering and persecutions in the centuries that followed, the history of anti-semitism. He ended with this statement: "The only solution for us is the re-establishment of a Jewish state. Only then will the real image of the Jew be restored and will the Jews become equal citizens in the family of nations."

A hush fell on the room. The young faces were earnest, concentrating on every syllable. "Any questions?" our teacher asked.

"Yes," said one of the boys. "For two thousand years we were persecuted, killed, pillaged and deprived of our rights. Why didn't we fight? Where were our youth? And where are our equal rights here in Poland?"

"It's too late to go into that now," said the teacher. "I shall try to answer your question tomorrow."

A special tie, a sort of conspiracy, had been created between our teacher and ourselves. At home I gave vague replies to my parents' usual questions about the class but my mind churned with all I had heard that afternoon. I waited eagerly for the next session.

Next day I came early again. This time the teacher told us in great detail about the history of the Jews in Poland, how they arrived in eastern Europe in the sixteenth century, and how gradually their situation had worsened until in 1934 Poland concluded a pact of friendship with Nazi Germany, and Joseph Goebbels, the Nazi Minister of Propaganda, was invited to lecture in the universities of Poland as the guest of the government. As long as Marshal Pilsudsky, the liberator of Poland, was alive, he tried to curb anti-Jewish acts. But immediately after his death in 1935 the Jews were again persecuted through economic boycotts and limiting of their civil rights. "Now more than ever the only solution for us," said our teacher, "is to restore our own home; there we may do and behave as we deem best. Here they persecute and kill us . . . Maybe now you will understand why your parents are so afraid. Anti-semitism is prevalent and the danger is real. In Germany they are already killing Jews, and who can tell when it may happen here? So don't abuse your parents. They sense the danger. They know that already anti-semitism is reaching horrible proportions in Poland."

Chapter Four

A summer evening. My sister and I were already in bed when we suddenly heard a knock on the door. A friend of the family, a Pole, came in and asked to speak with my father. Such a mysterious visit, I thought. About ten minutes later I heard him say good night and leave. But my father looked worried; obviously the man had brought bad news of some sort. In fact, he had hurried in to warn us that a group of about fifty Poles were preparing an old-fashioned pogrom. They were armed with knives and sharp tools and intended to attack their Jewish neighbours for no reason other than hate and robbery. They would not hesitate to kill and would seize anything available and then trump up false accusations against us as an excuse for this act. Our friend had also been asked to join them but he had refused. He begged father not to divulge the source of his information, else he be condemned by his fellow-Poles and treated accordingly. Father honoured his request but made sure the news passed at once from Jew to Jew.

My mother quickly decided to dress us and send us to relatives in another city. We were to stay there until the storm blew over. Our grandmother and grandfather would come with us. My sister and I wept, protesting that we did not want to leave the family and go to a safe place. "If it is dangerous for you, why should we leave you? And what will we do by ourselves?" But our pleas went unheeded; we had to go. We started out that very evening.

Two days of worry and tension followed before we could return. Then we learned the situation had solved itself without bloodshed. A delegation of Jews informed the police of the impending disaster, hoping the law would prevent its taking place. They were told to block all entrances to their houses and stay inside. The pogrom was foiled for two reasons. It seems that some of the participants were dissatisfied with the projected division of the spoils and threatened not to take part in the assault. Even as their argument continued, the police issued a warning against rioting. They then realized that someone had informed on them to us and through us to the police, and they cancelled the whole plan.

Most of the initiators were drunkards and petty hoodlums, including a number of hard-pressed coal-miners, who were easily influenced by anti-semitic propaganda because it provided them with scapegoats on whom they could hang their miserable lot.

But this episode served to immerse us in permanent fear. I had the feeling that we were surrounded by a wall, slowly suffocating, and that we must do something to liberate ourselves. But what could I do at my age? When I grow up, I resolved, I will never, never remain here, though it is my birthplace. I was born in Poland, as were my parents and grandparents before me, but this is not our home. It was about this time that I began to feel that the town, so dear to me, had become unbearably alien, a place in which it was impossible for me to survive.

The discussions at the Hebrew class, the atmosphere at home, and the attitude in our public school combined to make me feel I had to be constantly alert, to keep my eyes open and listen to every conversation, an attitude far beyond the ken of a girl of ten. I was not the only one to react this way. Many of the boys and girls of my age thought and felt similarly. We were all frustrated and bitter, burning with a wish to vent our dreams. We did not dream of dolls and bicycles but of packing up and going away, far, far from where we lived. I knew at that time that only through knowledge and education could I open the gates to the big, wide world, and that put my dream even further away for I would have to wait many years before I had learned enough. Why can't my whole family pack up and move away right now? I kept asking myself. What had they to lose? These questions gave me no peace.

Gradually I turned into a morose, introverted child and all my vivacity and love of life petered out. I became so sensitive that every slight injustice tortured me. I still took part in the games of my Polish girlfriends simply to forget my problems, but it was only a temporary appeasement. I could not adjust myself to the life of children who did not belong to the "special race" of Jews.

And then something happened that gave me hope. One beautiful spring day, the weather was mild and flocks of birds were returning from warmer countries. Their chirping and fluttering filled the air. Trees began to blossom and the air was filled with fragrance. Walking slowly home I noticed our neighbour's daughter, all smiles, singing to herself as she carried two big suitcases out of the house. "Hello!" I cried. "Are you going on a vacation?" "No," she called out happily, "one week from today I am leaving Poland! I'm going to Palestine." And she was gone, with the gate swinging shut behind her.

I felt terribly envious. I asked my mother. "Why can't we do that too? What have we got to lose?" Then all my secret dreams poured out. "Why can't we go to Palestine? We live all the time in fear. We are not safe here or at the synagogue. At school they hurt me. Whenever grandpa and grandma go out for a walk someone has to go with them, to keep boys from throwing stones at them. In the trains we are discriminated against. Our shops are picketted. At the universities they will accept only a few Jews and it is the same in the government— only a few Jews can get ahead. We are forced to be pedlars and shopkeepers with only our wits to keep us alive. Mother, how can we stand it any longer?"

It was a long speech for a child, and my mother answered me hesitantly, perhaps because she knew I was right. "Many Jews would like to leave Poland, but nobody lets us in anywhere...."

"But that's not fair! Why should some be privileged and others not? My friend is packed and ready to go. She leaves for Palestine in a week."

Mother again answered slowly. "Well, she has been taking special training . . . Only a few people are allowed to go, and only those who are trained in agriculture so they can develop the land." She knew she could not give me the answers I wanted. "I'm afraid you are too young to understand, dear. One day you will see for yourself."

Her answer did not satisfy me. But the year was 1939. Soon events occurred that shook the world and wrought destruction for the Jews of Poland. I could not think again about these questions until many months had passed.

Chapter Five

The year 1939 began with Hitler's declaration in a speech to the Reichstag that a new war in Europe would spell the extinction of the Jewish people. This ominous pronouncement was discussed, analyzed and interpreted by everyone, each in accord with his own circumstances and state of mind. The poor did not have time to speculate and forecast; they were too busy toiling for bread. Life could not be much harder for them than it already was, Hitler or no, they thought. The religiously-minded consoled themselves with the faith that God would not abandon His people if they trusted in Him. They were certain Hitler would meet the same end as Haman of old, and that Jewry would ultimately celebrate his downfall too. The wealthy did not attach much significance to the dictator's declaration because they were confident their money would keep them safe. Although they had the means to leave Poland, they preferred to remain to keep track of their business interests. Those who wanted to leave, the poor and lower middle class, lacked the means as well as entry permits into other countries. There were even some optimists who did not believe the Germans capable of implementing such a barbaric plan. Hitler's threats, they said, were just talk . . . The sum total was a passive waiting, although the flames were approaching rapidly. Opinions among us were so divided that only a very great leader could have united us. We foresaw the future in the treatment of the Jews in Germany, Austria and Czechoslovakia and had time to prepare for the emergency. But there was no such leader. We forgot that

"God helps those who help themselves" and only prayed to be saved.

The Nazis, however, were not idle. In one night thousands of Polish Jews, citizens of Poland living in Germany, were driven out of Germany across the border into Poland without being permitted to take anything with them. This was carried out methodically. The lists were carefully prepared. The raids were made in the middle of the night, with hundreds of SS breaking into Jewish homes all over Germany and forcing the half-naked, barefooted victims with kicks and beatings to climb into waiting trucks which brought them to the Polish border. There they were compelled to climb down and start walking into Polish territory. Shivering with cold, exhaustion and shock, and carrying babies in their arms, they arrived among us.

Sosnowiec was near the German border, in an area known as Oberschlesien, or Upper Silesia, and we were immediately aware of these new events. Germany's military might was a matter of common knowledge. The Munich Pact and the rape of Czechoslovakia were known to young and old. All of us, Jews and Poles alike, lived in a perpetual state of preparation for war. The use of poison gas was expected, and school children were instructed in making makeshift gasmasks. There were daily air raid alarms and frequent runs to the hastily built shelters. Fear, panic, and confusion reigned. Our school days became intolerable. The regular lessons were replaced by endless instructions on how to behave in case of war, air raids, gas attacks and the like. We learned to administer first aid and to go to the shelters quietly and in order. Instead of calming us, these activities increased our anxiety and our hearts pounded in panic all through the school hours.

I was happy when Friday afternoon arrived, welcoming the two days of peace at home and celebrating the Sabbath, the Jew's traditional day of rest. Friday night my father always went to the synagogue and all of us wore our Sabbath clothes. We ate at a table covered with a white cloth, the Sabbath candles alight, and the red sweet wine of sanctification in its bottle. Mother, her head covered with a beautiful kerchief, used to pray over the candles and we all felt so good and secure, at least for a short while. Father always brought a guest with him from the prayer service who, upon entering, blessed us all. My sister and I sometimes giggled and whispered to each other, making fun of our guest, and mother would rebuke us for forgetting our manners. It was normal, natural fun.

One Friday I felt that something was different. Special preparations were in progress, and they aroused my curiosity. "Mother," I asked, "are we having guests tonight?"

"Yes, dear, we've invited a family that was driven out of Germany to come to dinner and tea. We want to befriend them and hear what happened to the Jews in Germany. So please, behave yourselves!"

Next day I helped set the table for three more people. Father returned from the synagogue accompanied by a couple with a boy of nine. The woman was attractive, about thirty years old, with dark hair and eyes and an expression of fright which was clearly the result of what she had been through. The man was a bit older, tired looking and wearing clothes that were obviously not his own but had been given him by some kind soul. The boy spoke only German and had perfect manners, quite different from ours. My parents welcomed them warmly and did their best to make them feel at home.

"We are very happy to have you with us, Mr. and Mrs. Stern,"

said Mother as they shook hands. "We are honoured to have you in our home." We all felt that we should encourage them, make them realize they were not struggling alone. The old Jewish tradition, born of much suffering and misery, came to the fore: we must help the needy and reach out to the downtrodden. I recall vividly the tear-filled eyes of some neighbours, themselves wretchedly poor, when members of the Society for Helping German Refugees did not ask them for a contribution of clothing for the Nazi victims. They too wanted to do something to help.

After dinner a few of our friends drifted in to meet the couple and ask questions. The Sterns began to talk of their expulsion from Germany. "Is it true," someone asked, "that a civilized country like Germany has turned into a real madhouse?"

"You cannot imagine what is going on—it is beyond human understanding," Mr. Stern answered. "We are chased like beasts. These so-called civilized peoples have turned into bloodthirsty monsters, looking for scapegoats. We are outlaws and have no rights. They have seized all our property, our factories, our stores and businesses, our personal things, our homes. They attack us in the streets and even in our houses. Hitler is carrying out exactly what he promised in 'Mein Kampf'. He is preparing for war and needs money and raw materials and these he hopes to get from the Jews. The fact that other nations have not protested only encourages him."

The room was still. Everyone was submerged in thought. After a moment's pause, Mr. Stern said, "Let me tell you, as an example, about two neighbours, one a Jew, the other a Christian, who lived in the same building. Their children grew up together, the women went shopping together, and every day at five o'clock they had tea together. In other words—complete friendship. Until one day Fritz put on his uniform. Then, in his eyes, his Jewish friend turned into his worst enemy. One night Fritz and two other German soldiers knocked at his friend's door. The Jew invited him in. But instead of a friendly greeting Fritz cursed him like a dog. 'Get up, you dirty Jew, I don't know you at all. You are the enemy of the Third Reich. Pack a bag and within ten minutes be ready to go with us! ' Such things happen every day. A cultured nation turned overnight into a preying beast. The terrible shock of all this caused a wave of suicides among Jews, especially the intellectuals, who were rounded up and sent to concentration camps because Hitler and his hoodlums considered them the most dangerous element."

When he paused, Mrs. Stern said, "Take Dr. Klein. He was a prominent surgeon in Germany, a devoted man who gave most of his life to his patients. He would help any suffering human being. One morning one of his own patients, a man whose life he had saved, broke into Klein's home destroying and demolishing everything and then arrested the whole family and dragged them off without the slightest pity or remorse . . . Yes, that is how it is in Germany today; that is the naked truth."

Those present listened, their fear and distress mounting by the moment. The questions they finally began to ask must have seemed almost childish, but in their anxiety over their own destiny they simply couldn't believe what they had heard. Someone asked, "Are religious Jews treated with more respect than free-thinking Jews? Are bearded Jews in caftans and skull caps treated worse than shaven modern ones? "

The Sterns started to answer at the same time. "All Jews are alike for the Nazis! " And then Mr. Stern elaborated: "Assimilated Jews, even half-Jews, are as unlucky as any other Jew. Our *young people, those who were born in Germany and considered themselves German in every way, suffered most of all. They simply could not understand what had happened, why they were being persecuted, and many of them preferred to kill themselves rather than submit to further humiliation."*

"It is incredible, impossible!" someone whispered hoarsely.

"It is credible and possible!" cried Mr. Asher, one of my father's friends. He was an old, highly educated man, a close friend of our family. "It has happened in our history before." The Sterns both nodded in agreement.

"What do you think was our mistake?" someone asked timidly.

"As a German Jew," Mr. Stern replied thoughtfully, "according to my experience, I would say that our most serious mistake was that we tried to ignore our real identity. It's wrong to bring up children without roots, without tradition, without the sense of belonging to an ancient people with a rich history and culture. Had we not forgotten this, no Hitler in the world could have succeeded in breaking us."

At this point my mother, wishing to ease the tension, said softly, "It's time for tea now. Please come to the table." Cakes and fruits were set out, and all the guests ate and drank eagerly. "How quickly they go to the table," I thought to myself. "They want so much to forget the horror for a little while."

So engrossed was everyone in what was being said that they did not even notice that I was sitting there the whole time, drinking in every word, my heart racing with fright and shock. I did not understand the reality of their words, but I was instinctively aware of danger—the Nazi terror could visit my home too. I did not think of leaving this conversation to play outside with my friends as I usually did on Saturdays.

Soon everyone in Poland was talking about what the German refugees had revealed. This was the main, almost the only, topic of conversation in every Jewish household and wherever friends and neighbours gathered. People could hardly believe that such cruelty could exist in the enlightened twentieth century, and some even questioned the authenticity of the tales they heard. "They are exaggerating; they want to arouse sympathy." Again and again the same naive questions: Do Jews with traditional garments and beards suffer more? What about those who have converted to Christianity? What about mixed marriages? —as if, among these fine discriminations they could find reason to sidestep the all-encompassing hatred of Hitler.

And the answers, for us, were almost beyond credibility. We lived close to Germany, we knew, trusted and liked the German people and could not conceive of them performing such barbaric acts. Every refugee told, more or less, the same story. Women, who encouraged their husbands to join the Nazis hoping to make life easier for their families, were the first to be thrown into concentration camps. Men with Jewish wives who joined the SS would not spare their own spouses and children. Even people whose families had converted to Christianity three generations before were still considered Jews and treated accordingly, only they bitterly blamed the Jews for their fate and desperately tried to erase their antecedents' connections. But the long cudgels hit them and their children as well.

I listened without asking questions. Young as I was, I regretted having been born into such an age. Gradually I stopped playing with children of my age and took an interest only in listening to the conversations of the grownups. I read all the newspapers I could, especially articles about Hitler's plans to conquer Poland. The pictures in the press showed Nazi military parades with their modern and deadly equipment, and in everyone, young or old, fear grew.

People began hoarding foodstuffs, particularly flour, sugar, potatoes, beans, oil, soap, candles and matches. Very soon all the supplies vanished from shops and stores. My family was no exception. My father also prepared for the coming emergency, laying in a stock of all these items, plus a good supply of medicines and pills. Strange though it may seem, the activity of hoarding gave people a certain measure of self-assurance, as if it made them ready to face the imminent war. A special committee checked to see whether air raid shelters were available as they should be. Special classes in first aid were organized for adults, and people were trained to carry stretchers on the run as in real war conditions. Differences were pushed aside as Jews and Poles joined in these preparations for survival, but we knew that if war came we would become special targets, and in this our Polish friends did not share. We children went to school as usual, but there was no pretense of learning. All attention was devoted to war drills. We were tense, our nerves on edge, and even the hooting of an automobile horn in the street made us jump. When we learned of the Hitler-Stalin pact, we had no doubt that Germany would surely attack Poland. Every little noise seemed to us a falling bomb.

A small, unexpected measure of relief came when the Polish government issued a curious law obliging all home-owners to paint and repair the outsides of their houses and fences under pain of punishment. Immediately people embellished the law with their own hopeful interpretations. "If the government has time for such edicts," people would say, "the danger cannot be so great." Many were encouraged by the agreement that had been reached by England and Poland which promised that if Poland were attacked, England would come at once to her aid. There was endless speculation. Some claimed that all of Hitler's propaganda was "just bluff", while others insisted that he knew what he wanted and meant to get it. Still others remarked ironically that the houses were being beautified so that Hitler would like them when he conquered Poland, but it was a bitter joke at best.

Chapter Six

Summer came and with it the vacation. But how different it was this time! Nature alone remained unchanged: flowers were in bloom, filling the air with their entrancing fragrance; the sun rose and set as usual. But parents were worried and kept their offspring near them, fearful of what tomorrow might bring. I missed the Saturday hikes we used to have when we would pack food and drinks into our knapsacks and go off into the forests for a full day of fun. Although the walking was often rough, it was always lightened by happy singing and gay talk. The forest itself was always full in summer with adults and children enjoying themselves in the cool shade. While the grownups picked mushrooms, we used to gather blackberries, competing among ourselves to see who could pick the most and bring them to mother to bake into wonderful cakes. Sometimes we would surprise young lovers and frighten them from their romantic hideouts.

In the summer of 1939 the forests remained empty, such excursions into the woods were ruled out. There were no adults with free time on their hands and the necessary frame of mind to accompany us as they had in years past. We were happy, therefore, when Grandma Marcia, my father's mother, arrived from Keltz to visit us, as she did every year. She was a wonderful old lady, tiny, with blonde hair and light-coloured eyes. People often said she had the face of an angel, soft and gentle. She had the most delightful sense of humour and we loved her very much. So it was with great anticipation that we went to the railway station to meet her one day toward the end of June. When the train came in and the passengers disembarked, we spied our grandmother. She looked very grave. Two of her sons had already been mobilized into the Polish army, and she was worried and sad. Day after day my sister and I tried to distract her, but to no avail. And then in August the postman brought us a registered letter: father was ordered to report the next day for mobilization with all the essential equipment.

Mother turned deathly pale and could scarcely speak. Then, after a hurried consultation, my parents decided that since we lived close to the German border, we were in peril. As a precaution, Grandma, my sister and I would leave at once for father's family home in Keltz, which was much further inside Poland and therefore, it seemed, safer.

My sister and I refused to leave, but the decision was final. We had to go. And at once. There was no time to waste. We immediately began to pack our things while mother packed father's knapsack. We could not swallow our food that evening but went to bed early.

The next morning we walked to the railroad station, where we embraced in tears. Father boarded the train bound for Warsaw and we the one going in the opposite direction, to the District of Keltz. Only mother remained behind, alone, crying her heart out. None of us knew when we would see one another again.

It had always been one of my dreams to travel far and wide, to see new cities with their historical relics and new, beautiful countryside. But of this trip nothing remains in my memory but the sadness in our hearts. The rolling green fields we saw from the train windows made no impression on us. I was indifferent to everything that might ordinarily have been of interest. The separation from my parents, my father's going off to war—these were my only thoughts. Nothing else mattered.

At the Keltz station we were met by my father's brother, an uncle my sister and I had not met before. He was around fifty and therefore too old for mobilization. He immediately made it clear how pleased they were to have us, showing great kindness and consideration, complimenting us both on how big we were, how pretty we had grown—but he could not lift our spirits. Himself the father of three handsome sons, he had always wanted a daughter, and this special tenderness was communicated in his relationship to us. He introduced us to his wife and sons and placed us at the table, where a fine meal was set for us. All of them did everything in their power to make us welcome and happy, but all we could think about was our separation from our parents. Would we ever see them again?

We had been there only two weeks when, on the first of September, the radio announced that the Germans had crossed the Polish borders. They had invaded Poland. The war was on. The news shocked everyone, in spite of all our preparations. The terror of the Nazis, Hitler's repeated declarations about the final solution of the Jewish problem—nobody really knew yet what he meant by it—made us all fearfully apprehensive, but our first reaction was bewilderment, confusion. Our main fear was of bombs. Everyone was certain that cities and towns would be the first targets, so it seemed wisest to pack some things and run for the villages. Surely the Germans would not waste their bombs on scattered houses, an old stable, or a shack belonging to a sharecropper! Polish patriots even boasted that the Polish army was sure to defeat the Germans and return everything to normal once again. After all, they argued, the British were coming to our aid, and who could defeat the British Empire?

Some even went so far as to plan victory celebrations. But when the first German war planes appeared high above the town and the sirens began to shriek, everyone ran panic-stricken for the air raid shelters.

When the all-clear sounded and we emerged, my uncle said, "There's not a minute to lose. We must pack and start moving!" He hired a horse and a cart from a farmer; we packed hastily and started out. Only my grandmother, my sister and I rode, perched on top of the luggage; the others walked. We saw on the road thousands of people, many carrying children, many old men and women, all looking for safety. The young men had, of course, been mobilized for military service. It was a mass flight with no one knowing precisely where to go. The lucky ones, like ourselves, had a horse and wagon—the only means of transport at the time—but the great majority were running away on foot. People were fleeing in every direction, for the German army seemed to be everywhere at once. We created an instant bond with our fellow-citizens on the road, exchanging what information we had willingly. This great mass movement had no order, no destination, but we were united as one in our desperate desire to get away from the Germans.

After an exhausting day we came upon a deserted stable and, entering it, dropped on the ground and slept. Another day we were fortunate enough to find a house whose owner had left it hurriedly to seek refuge elsewhere. We wandered thus for six days. One night, when we were still not very far out, for travel by foot is slow indeed, we found refuge in the home of a kind sharecropper. Others too came knocking at his door and soon the house was packed wall to wall. That night the German Luftwaffe bombed the town. The panic was unbelievable; women hid their children under beds and inside closets, as if this would keep them safe from the hell that was dropping from above. My

47

sister and I instinctively looked for our aunt and stood motionless against her. It was the first time we had ever heard bombs exploding. We were frozen with fear.

The next morning my uncle gathered us together and we were on our way again. At the end of six nerve-wracking days we realized there was nowhere to go. Wherever we turned, the Nazis had preceded us, sowing havoc and destruction ruthlessly as they went. The wishful thinking of the Polish patriots was proved wrong. With heavy hearts and broken spirits people started returning home. We did the same.

On our way back we saw the first victims of German barbarism. Simply to sow terror, the Nazis had picked groups at random, accused them of treason or sabotage and killed them, strewing their bodies along the roads. Sometimes they even stuck weapons into the luggage of the wandering refugees to "prove" their guilt. Our group, at least, was lucky enough to make it back home.

Life was now painfully lonely for my sister and I. We longed for our parents, the comfort and warmth of their presence, and our own home. Our sadness was increased when we could hear from afar the rumbling of the German war machine approaching, as if to grind us to dust. The sound made the blood freeze in our veins. We were afraid to go out, and if we did step outside the house for a moment, the mere sight of a German soldier in the distance made us scurry back like frightened mice.

At that time, the question that was uppermost in our minds was news of our parents. But there was none. All communications had been cut. The post and telegraph stopped functioning. There was no alternative but to wait. We stood for hours at the window, watching, wondering, perhaps . . . ? Whenever the door opened we jumped to our feet full of hope, but alas, it was always the same people.

Chapter Seven

On that first day of September, when the Germans invaded Poland, people who lived near the border fled their homes helter-skelter in a frenzy of fear. They went wherever their feet carried them. Whole villages along the border were emptied of their occupants in a matter of hours, and, passing through, one could see chickens, geese and ducks roaming about and dogs barking wildly at the passers-by. After a few days, when the people discovered there was no escaping the Germans, they wearily returned to their homes.

As we learned later, it was while wandering with such a group fleeing from the borders that my mother happened to meet two men, a father and a son, both businessmen from the Keltz district, who had started out on a business trip before the invasion and were now bent on returning home. She decided to go with them so as to be with us. The first two days they were quite lucky; for a few miles they were even given a lift in a carriage. Whenever they were stopped and their papers checked they managed to pass without arousing suspicion. At night they found shelter in deserted houses. Because of the curfew that had been imposed, they had to find a place for the night early in the afternoon, but the people they encountered were helpful and kind.

On the third day of their travels they were stopped by two German soldiers. This time the Germans checked their papers *thoroughly, and when they found they were Jews, the soldiers shouted furiously, "Off to headquarters, you dirty Jewish traitors, foreign agents!"*

With their knees shaking and in a cold sweat, my mother and the two men were propelled into a school building the Nazis had taken over for the headquarters of the local German unit. One of the two soldiers opened the door, raised his arm in the Heil Hitler salute and announced, "I've just caught some Jews, traitors and enemies of the Third Reich." The father and son were brutally beaten and thrown into a cell, where they were held for twenty-four hours without food or drink and were interrogated for hours on end. They were so frightened they could scarcely speak a word in their own defense. Every question brought a fresh torrent of abuse and blows, accompanied by shouts of "dirty Jew!", "Schweinhund!", and the like.

Mother was treated much better, mainly because she spoke fluent German and also perhaps because she did not show outward signs of fear. With dignity and courtesy she tried to explain that there must be some misunderstanding. "We are not traitors," she declared. "I don't even know what a foreign agent is. I'm a simple housewife, and I know these two gentlemen to be decent and honest citizens who work hard." "Sir," she appealed to the officer, "I see that you are an educated and intelligent man. Could you imagine that with their limited education these two men could be anything more than candy salesmen or something similar? They are very simple people with large families to support. As for myself, I am certainly no Mata Hari, and nobody would dream of offering me such a job . . . They were on a business trip and unable to get a train home, that is why we are making our way on foot."

"And what about you, where are you going? Where is your

husband?" asked the officer, who fortunately was a Wehrmacht officer, a military man, and not a member of the terrorists, the SS or Gestapo.

"My children are spending their vacation, as they do every year, with their grandmother in Keltz. Quite by chance I met these two men and, as we were all going in the same direction, I joined them so that I might bring my children home."

The officer observed mother closely, and then he asked, "How do you happen to know German so well? And where is your husband?" Naturally, mother refrained from informing him that father was serving in the Polish army. Instead she said he was ill and had to stay at home. As for her German, she studied it at school. Thus the investigation ended and she was taken back to the guard room. The officer ordered that the three be given food and drink. Then they waited twelve hours for his verdict. They could not close their eyes all night. What would happen to them? Would they never see their families again?

Early the next morning they heard the heavy steps of a soldier approaching. Their hearts almost stopped beating. The door was opened and the soldier read aloud the officer's decision: my mother was to be released but the two men were to remain in custody.

But mother did not lose her head. She insisted that she could not leave alone, she felt responsible for the men, she did not know her way on foot, and she demanded to see the commanding officer again—all in fluent German.

Several hours elapsed. The three waited in silence, too tense to speak. At last mother was brought before the officer once more. "It is lucky for you," he remarked, "that I am a German officer.

I believed you and now I cannot understand why you refuse my offer of freedom."

"I do thank you, sir, but please believe me, they are not spies and I beg you to release them." At this point she could not contain herself any longer and broke into tears. "They are not foreign agents; please, please, release them too." The officer did not reply but merely motioned to the orderly to escort mother back to the guard room.

More frightening hours passed until, in the early evening, the three of them were finally released and they went on their way. The two men, whom in fact my mother had not known personally before, thanked her over and over again for her courage and concern for their safety. "We have never seen such a brave and wonderful woman!"

At the time this was happening my sister and I were still with our relatives in Keltz, quite ignorant of these dramatic events and of our mother's whereabouts. Day followed day and my sister developed the habit of crying. "I want mother! I want her to come right now!" she sobbed, and she seemed to find relief in doing so.

Chapter Eight

Early one evening after sunset, when the sky was dark with clouds and a light drizzle obscured our view of the road, we were sent to bed. Worn out with another day of watching and waiting, we fell asleep almost immediately. And then our mother entered. We did not hear anything. Everyone was overjoyed to see her and told her everything that had happened. She asked them not to wake us but tiptoed into our room to look at us as we lay sleeping.

In the morning our aunt came in, all smiles, and hurried us with the words, "Get up and dress quickly, girls! I have a surprise for you, but hurry!" She took us to the room where mother was still asleep. "Don't wake her!" she urged, but that was beyond our powers of restraint. Seeing mother at last we whooped with joy and her eyes flew open. We kissed and hugged her and hopped up and down excitedly. Too tired to get up, mother begged after a while to be allowed to sleep a bit longer. But we did not leave her room, staying as close to her as we could without disturbing her rest. The feeling that she might disappear again unconsciously took hold of us, and we knew—how well we knew!—that only in her presence could we be happy. Drawn, exhausted and emaciated as she was, she was our image of love and devotion.

Rest, however, was brief. Concern for father's fate gave mother no peace. At the end of a week's stay, when her badly swollen *feet had returned to normal and her unnaturally pale face had taken on a more rosy look, we packed again for our return home. There we would await father's coming. All of my uncle's pleas not to go on foot, not to be forced to lodge in a barn or stable, not to run the risk of being caught by the Germans, could not deter us from going home. We bade all our relatives goodbye and started out.*

For more than a mile we trudged along with our packs, turning our heads frequently to see our relatives still standing there sadly waving to us until a bend in the road removed them from our view. We could not know that morning in 1939 that we would never see any of them again.

We walked steadily on, stopping now and then beside the road to rest our feet and refresh ourselves with the food and drink we had brought along. Toward evening we persuaded one of the sharecroppers to take us in for the night. Next morning we were lucky enough to find another farmer who agreed, for a fee, to take us in his wagon to the next village. Occasionally people riding by in a horse-drawn cart would give us a lift without payment.

It was slow going. I kept asking when we would reach home and always received the same reply: "Soon! " And finally—the "soon" materialized. Our own street, the same trees, bare now because autumn had come and their leaves lay golden-brown on the ground, the same houses, stores and apartment buildings. But the usually busy streets were empty; the rare few who were out looked nervous and frightened. The atmosphere was heavy and tense. But we were happy to be home and to find my mother's family all there to welcome us. Every little detail of our apartment sent a thrill of joy through me, as if we had been away from each other for a long, long time. But there was one thing terribly missing—father. There was no sign of him, not a letter or a postcard, nothing.

Even before we could rest our sore feet we were showered with questions, and we hurled many of our own. Thankfully we learned that all the family was in good health. We then washed, ate something and went straight to bed. In no time we were fast asleep.

We were so tired we didn't wake up until late the next morning. During breakfast mother glanced out the window and suddenly recoiled in shock. "What's the matter?" I cried. Mother patted my shoulder to quiet me. "I've just seen Mrs. Finkel in mourning clothes," she answered. "I must find out. If, God forbid, something has happened I must try to console her." We dressed quickly and went to ask our aunt and uncle in the next apartment. Mother's instinct had been right. Something really terrible had happened to the Finkels. Although our flight had been hard and filled with danger, the plight of those who remained in the city had been far worse.

When the Germans had entered our town on that September 1, there had been no army to resist their invasion. They came rushing in with blood-curdling shouts and shrieks. All the inhabitants shut themselves up in their homes, terrified by the leaping and screaming "mad Nazi dogs", who were running up and down the streets looking for victims. Through the night the people remained hidden in the cellars and dark corners of their houses. Then early in the morning two shots were heard—later the Germans claimed they had been fired on from two houses—whereupon they broke into all the houses on the street, driving everyone out. They kept the male Jews sixteen to seventy years old and allowed the rest to go back into their homes. An hour later they ordered all Jewish males to report to an appointed *place. Failure to report meant instant death.*

Hundreds of men were then forced into one small stifling hall. Shouts, kicks and blows drove them inside. Then came alternate orders to lie down and get up, stand still and run on the spot, raise hands with faces to the wall—all in quick succession. Anyone who could not comply was beaten mercilessly, many to death. So much blood flowed that the town hall looked like a slaughter-house. No one was permitted a single drop of water in the heat and congestion of that wretched mass. Toward evening the men were ordered outside and commanded to run with their hands raised. Behind their backs the sound of machine guns was heard. Instinctively many ducked to avoid the shots, and these were punished at once with blows. "Get on your knees and stay there!" Whoever moved was again beaten savagely. The men were kept in this position for hours, going into their second day without anything to drink or eat. Suddenly they were ordered to get up and run as shots were fired above their heads. The old and crippled, who could not run, were beaten or shot to death. Then the Nazis took the first ten men inside the hall and shot them. The bodies strewn in the courtyard were also dragged inside. The rest were now commanded to lie on their stomachs without moving and remained thus until dawn, when they were suddenly given water to drink. Now the Nazis selected sixty men and ordered them to dig a shallow ditch. Thirty were then shot and buried in that ditch—the rest of the men in the courtyard were sent home. "Yes," my uncle said, "everything was done methodically and thoroughly, with the famous German efficiency." One of the thirty men shot was Mrs. Finkel's husband. She was now a widow with five small children.

"How," my mother gasped, "could any human being be so cruel to another who had done him no harm?" She voiced the

thought in all our minds. But my uncle replied broodingly, "That is what we all ask ourselves. But it seems there is a beast hidden deep within people. When awakened it knows no human kindness. Ask those who witnessed the slaughter; the German soldiers seemed to be enjoying it...."

We were silent for a very long time. Nobody wanted to speak.

Chapter Nine

Still no word from father. Our anxiety increased with every day that passed. Polish soldiers were returning from the front. Whenever someone we knew came back, we hurried over to ask whether by some chance he had seen father or heard anything about him. But no one had any news for us. The days turned into weeks. Poland lay conquered, though fighting still continued in Warsaw. We were still waiting. There was no one to ask anymore, nothing to be done. We could only hope that one day he would open the door and be there.

Late one night, there was a knock on the door. Ah, we thought excitedly, father! To our great disappointment, however, it was not father but a friend who had served in the same unit with him. We asked him in and plied him with questions: Why had father not returned with him? Where had he seen father last and when? Was he all right?

Patiently Mr. Stachek answered that they had last been together near the town Chelm. Their officers had then informed them that Poland had been occupied by the Germans and that they were being sent home as soon as a train was available. He himself had not waited for the train but, obtaining civilian clothes in a neighbouring village, had gone forth on his own. He was sure father was coming too.

Time dragged on until, again, one night there was a knock on the door. This time we didn't jump up with joy; we asked, "Who is it?" It was father. We were together again, and we hoped against hope it would be for good. No one slept a wink that night. We sat listening to his stories, thankful that he was safe and well, for so many of his friends had died. The fact of the matter was that he had not seen much actual fighting. Each day brought them new orders for retreat until they reached the town of Chelm. There the commanders revealed Poland's defeat and the partition of Poland contrived by Hitler and Stalin. The Polish soldiers were released and were free to go home. The officers did advise, however, that they wait for specially scheduled trains since other transportation was scarce. Most of the men were at the point of exhaustion and agreed. They welcomed the possibility of travelling home by train rather than making their way on foot. The great majority, therefore, entered the railroad cars when they pulled up and soon fell asleep. But when they awoke, they saw that they were travelling in the opposite direction, toward the Soviet Union! They had been tricked by their own officers. My father and another soldier immediately decided to jump off the moving train. "We've not a minute to lose," father cried. "We're getting further and further from home!" Leaving their knapsacks behind, the two jumped. They were only slightly injured and, by helping each other, managed to reach a nearby village, where they knocked at the door of a sharecropper's hut, told their story and were welcomed inside and given civilian clothes. The man's wife attended to their injuries and gave them food. Then they threw away everything that could prove they were soldiers, and after a good night's sleep, they took sturdy sticks to lean on and started out on foot.

Dawn was approaching when father finished his story. Again we embraced and kissed each other. For a moment the conquerors were forgotten, so happy were we in the miracle of my father's return.

Chapter Ten

We had survived the invasion, our family was intact. Now we got down to the serious business of staying alive, for the Germans ruled with a steel fist. Having implanted terror and fear in the public-at-large to cow any thought of insurrection, they proceeded, methodically, to work on the Jews. They issued a new edict every other day isolating us from the rest of the Poles: formal notice was served that we were a race apart. On September 8, shortly after the invasion, the Germans ordered that every Jewish shop must be marked by a yellow Star of David, every Jewish identity card by a yellow stripe. On November 20, to cite another example, all bank accounts belonging to Jews were frozen and blocked. Before the end of the year all Jews were ordered to deliver for German confiscation all cars, radio sets, bicycles, telephones, and cameras. By that time too, every Jew aged ten or over was obliged to wear a white armband with a blue Star of David in the centre. Jews were not allowed to leave their homes between seven o'clock in the evening and five o'clock in the morning; this curfew was strictly enforced and woe to the Jew who ventured out. All Jewish schools were closed and the public schools, of course, had to expel Jewish pupils.

Simultaneously the Nazis proceeded to kill off any individuals they could get their hands on who were likely to cause them trouble, especially spiritual leaders, well-known rabbis, and leading intellectuals. They destroyed cultural centres *and burned down synagogues—sometimes with the devout still in them, burning them alive. The SS broke into private homes, accused intellectuals of imaginary crimes and put them to death after the most brutal tortures. Some of these special people singled out for persecution and death succeeded in fleeing to the Russian-occupied sectors of Poland; others went underground and fought the enemy in that way. Anyone who had the potential for stirring the masses was put on a list; searches and arrests became an everyday occurrence. If the person sought was not at home, family and friends were taken instead—and never heard of again. Being taken away for investigation became associated with certain death. As a result, people began to flee in the direction of the Russian sectors. Whole families were running for their lives.*

In a very short time the killing of Jews became an everyday phenomenon. Gone were my feelings of rebellion, my demand for solutions to injustice. I clung to my family. The succession of edicts and the relentless persecution and killing of Jews did not give us a moment to draw a free breath. We, like so many other families, gathered together for an earnest family consultation. It was decided—after the adults had considered the developments of the first few months of the war, and had weighed our chances for survival—that it might be best for us to flee to Soviet Russia. But grandfather objected strongly. After he had heard everyone out, he took the floor to have his say. "Children," he declared gravely, "I do not for one moment believe we can find safe refuge with people who made a non-aggression pact with Germany. Before the negotiations, Stalin dismissed his foreign minister, Litvinoff, supposedly because he refused to have anything to do with an alliance with Hitler's Germany; but I think he was dismissed simply because he was a Jew. At any rate, it pleased Hitler very much, as you probably read in the newspapers. Germany and Russia divided the spoils of Poland after the German invasion. No, I do not think we can find peace among the Russians...."

Grandfather's arguments were persuasive; this was obvious in the faces of his listeners. The only one who did not agree with him was his son, my mother's only brother, who thought grandfather's attitude toward Russia was really based on painful memories of the past. He asked most respectfully to reply. "Father," he said, "I know how you feel because you were a witness to many pogroms in Russia, but things have changed since then. Russia is no longer the same, and our life under the Russians would certainly be safer than here with the Nazis."

"You are right, my son," answered grandfather. "Time has changed many things. But facts are facts; one cannot put his trust in these people. They will betray us as they betrayed their own people by joining with the Nazis. I could never trust them—never!"

We arrived at no decision. The family scattered, everyone going to his own home, sadder, more confused and worried than before.

In the meantime more edicts were enacted: Jews were not permitted on trains, and their use of street cars was strictly limited. They were systematically driven out of the small towns and villages and concentrated in large centres, being allowed to take only a few belongings with them. The small towns were then declared "Judenrein", clean of Jews. The first to be driven out of their homes were the Jews of the community of Auschwitz. They were brought to our town, and our community did all in its power to help them adjust to life in our midst.

Again the subject of flight was brought up. This time grandma had her say. Firmly she told grandfather that he could not take the responsibility for the fate of all his children and grandchildren; he must submit to the wish of the majority. And the majority wish was to flee. I for one was very pleased with this decision, for I had nothing whatever to do all day, having been expelled from school. Now that the decision had been made, preparations for our flight were made quickly. The one thing still lacking was a means of transport, and each of the men in our large family was trying to find it.

After a couple of days' effort, two of my uncles came home looking worn and ravaged. They looked at each other, and the elder of the two began to speak. "I am sorry," he said, "to disappoint you all, but it is much worse than we realized. I must tell you what we have learned about recent events at the border. The Nazi leaders asked the Soviets on the other side of the border to sign an agreement—any Jew fleeing this side and caught by the Russians must be turned over to the Germans in Poland, and vice versa. The agreement has been signed, and the frontier guards have received their instructions." He paused for a moment and then continued. "What we found out was that some people left Sosnowiec, just recently, knowing nothing of this agreement. There were ten of them and they managed to slip by the German guards and were then caught by the Russians on the other side. They thought the Russians would be friendly and didn't even try very hard to hide from them. When they learned they were going to be returned, they were horrified. The women fell to their knees, weeping and pleading with the Russians not to turn them over. 'Don't you know what they will do? They'll kill us all!' But nothing helped; they were turned over, and as they entered the demilitarized zone separating the two sides, they were gunned down and all were killed."

We were shocked. Some of the adults could not believe the

story. "Some people have been able to get through, I know it," one of my aunts said; and they went out to check the facts. This particular story was confirmed—and that was enough. We abandoned our plan of escape.

Grandfather remarked, though without vengeful motive, "Well, you see, I was right. But mark my words, there is not a people in the world that can safeguard its own interests for all time by sacrificing the Jews. This crime never pays. Remember this." We listened in glum despair, and grandfather, eager to encourage us, added, "Don't you worry, children. After all, we are simple, honest people. We have never broken any laws. I am nearly seventy and have never been to court. They have no reason to hurt us. They won't touch us." But, even as he spoke, a new edict was published which ordered every Jewish male, sixteen to forty years old, to report for forced labour for the Germans. And we soon had another reason to regard grandfather's speech with some irony.

It was not too much later, on a bitter cold night early in the winter, that we heard a car screech to a stop at our gate. Our family, including my grandparents and my aunts who lived in our building, were huddled together in one room trying to keep warm and save on fuel. Peeping through the frost-covered window, we saw four SS men armed to the teeth leap from the car and rush through the gate to our building. A few seconds later a rifle butt banged on our door, someone shouted "Open up!", and the four broke in.

Our faces were deathly pale. One of the Nazis unfolded a paper in his hand and barked out the name written there. It was grandfather's. He was to come with them. His daughters immediately began to plead to be taken in his place because "he is a sick old man", but in vain. "Get out of the way!" was the rude answer as the women were pushed roughly aside. "It's the old man we want! " What his crime was and where they were taking him they would not say. Grandfather took his coat and hat quietly, turned to face his family with a calm "Goodbye, children. God bless you", and he was gone, with the hardfaced SS surrounding him.

We stood as if frozen for a long moment. Then two of my aunts broke into sobs and the third hurried out to see what could be done to save him. First she went to the German police headquarters to try to discover what he was being accused of. There she learned that grandfather along with nine other old men, Poles among them, were to be held as hostages. They would be kept in custody until the gangster Stefan turned himself in or was caught. Failing this, all ten old men would be put to death. A notice to this effect was posted all over town. There was not a chance, we all sighed, that Stefan would give himself up voluntarily, and the possibilities of their catching him were just as slight.

This was a most paradoxical situation, for my grandfather not only knew the bandit but had, with reservations, a decided respect for him. I remembered the one time I had had the dubious pleasure of seeing this notorious fellow. It was shortly before the war. As I was walking with my grandfather one day, we met a tall young man with light blond hair and bright blue eyes. His broad-shouldered figure was dressed most elegantly. Grandfather greeted him cordially: "How are you, Mr. Stefan? I haven't seen you for a long time. How you have grown! What a handsome fellow you've become! "

The young man stopped. He acknowledged the compliments with an indifferent shrug, but added in a serious tone, "You are good neighbours, so you know you have nothing to fear *from me. I respect good neighbours and even defend them in time of need. If anyone does anything to harm you, just you let me know and I'll give him what is coming to him!" And he hurried off.*

"Grandpa," I had questioned wonderingly, "he's so young, yet he seems to be an important person." Grandfather burst into hearty laughter. "Yes, child, indeed yes! He is a very important person!" He laughed every time he recalled my naive comment. Now, as I remembered that incident, laughter seemed impossible. It was 1940 and my grandfather, whom Stefan had promised to defend, was a hostage for Stefan himself. Now I I wanted to find out more about this man, and set about making inquiries of my relatives and neighbours.

It seems that when he was young, Stefan and his parents lived in the next building to us, in a poor attic room. His father worked in the coal mines and his pay was good, but he spent it on drink. He was a chronic alcoholic, a slave to vodka. His wife found consolation in the company of other men. Stefan was their only son, a bright, golden-haired boy, and he quickly became a problem child. At school he spent most of his hours out in the corridor because he was constantly disturbing the teachers and getting into scrapes with other children. The teachers simply couldn't handle him. But he was very intelligent, physically strong and well-developed for his age. Even as a child he had organized a gang of young ruffians who attacked other children, demanding money and beating up those who either resisted or had none to give. The parent's complaints became so numerous that the principal had to expel Stefan.

The boy grew into one of the most famous outlaws in our district. Such prowess and skill was attributed to him that his fame spread far and wide and he became the stuff of legends. The mere mention of his name was inclined to arouse fear. Still, he retained an affection for his old neighbourhood and respected the people who had been "good neighbours" to him. He never threatened them in any way and was even known to quietly help them out if they needed it. The police arrested him now and again, but were never able to prove anything conclusive against him because the actual crimes were committed by his henchmen, and Stefan kept his own hands clean. When the Nazi authorities tried to track him down, with every German soldier carrying his photograph in his pocket, Stefan outwitted them by changing his appearance every few days: now he was a priest, now a beggar, a nun, a farmer, and so on, with such skill that they were never able to catch him. They tried closing off streets and whole neighbourhoods when they heard he was in the area. Stefan was a thorn in the Nazis' flesh; he was one of the few outlaws who refused to co-operate with the German invaders but opposed them consistently. They were in a frenzy to get their hands on him. Finally, they took ten men hostage in the hope that Stefan's well-known gallantry might impel him to turn himself in.

But he did not. We were dreadfully frightened, but they did not kill the hostages after all. They released the men at the end of one week and instead published a large photograph of Stefan, offering a huge sum to the person whose help would lead to his arrest. This succeeded. An informer squealed and the Nazis surrounded the cave where he was hiding with tanks, heavy artillery and machine guns. Realizing there was no hope, Stefan drew his gun and killed himself. A picture of the dead Stefan appeared next day in every newspaper with the warning: "This will be the end of anyone who dares defy the German authorities! " . . . but no mention was made of his final, defiant gesture.

Chapter Eleven

The Nazis declared one town or village after another Judenrein. At first these transfers of people did not arouse much apprehension in us. We thought the Germans were only making their forced labour arrangements more efficient by concentrating Jews in the more easily administered larger centres. And, of course, it was sheer robbery. Allowed to carry only a few belongings with them, about forty-five pounds, the remainder of their property was grabbed by the Germans. Everything moveable and valuable, like furniture, jewelry and clothes, was shipped to Germany. The rest was given to the local Poles, thus solidifying their relationship with the Nazis. How well the Germans understood the nature of the uneducated, the poverty-stricken, and the psychology of the long history of Polish persecution of the Jews. They offered the majority of the Poles something too tempting to resist.

More and more of these refugees from other communities came to Sosnowiec, families and individuals looking for a personal haven. Among them was a man I remember in particular. He became famous for his ability to tell the future by reading the palms of people's hands. He did not charge much, only one zloty, and was in such great demand that one had to wait weeks for one's turn. This was not surprising under the circumstances. Beset by such awesome dangers on all sides, everyone yearned for a sign of what the future held in store for him, each one desperately hoping for some good news. Many of our young men and women had been accused by the Nazis of being communists and were arrested on this pretext; their wives, sweethearts and mothers were anxious for word that they would soon be released and returned to their homes. The lovelorn hoped to be told of coming romances and marriages.

I might not have known about this man at all, had it not been for my mother's younger sister, my aunt Bronka. She was about twenty-four at the time. Her fiance had been jailed for a petty misdeed, and she was eager to go to the palmist but wanted mother to accompany her. Mother refused; she did not believe in fortune-telling or other guesswork. "Only God determines our fortunes," she declared, "and He does not disclose them in advance." "Indeed," said my aunt, "we do believe in God, but don't you think that just out of curiosity it's worth meeting such a person? A man who chose for himself such a strange profession may reveal at least something about the past if not the future . . . ." "All right," said my mother, seeing the importance of this visit to her sister.

When their turn came, they found the visit was quite a ritual. Each had to place her money on the table, take a seat opposite the palmist and stretch out her hand, palm up. After staring at my mother's hand for a long time, he handed her back her money. "Why?" mother asked.

"I cannot tell you anything today," the palmist replied. "There is always a day in the year during which one's lines are blurred, and I cannot then tell the person's fortune. But do have tea with me." Mother accepted his invitation. During tea he asked her many questions: was she married? how old was she? how many children did she have and what were their ages? would she like to go to some other place for a time, and in that case was there someone who could look after her daughters? Then

he wished her all the best and told her she need not come back; everything would be all right.

When mother came home and described her visit to this man and how he had refused to take her money, we were a little bewildered, but since none of us put much faith in his ability to foresee the future, we soon forgot the incident. Later I was to recall it and wonder: did he really read my mother's future and know that she would need someone to look after her daughters?

Chapter Twelve

By now, all Jews had been deprived of any form of livelihood and were forbidden the normal commerce of keeping their homes supplied with the necessities of life. The members of our family were no exception. Having no alternative, we began to deal in the black market. Even my sister and I were given important tasks in this gruesome business.

We started by going to the villages a short way from our home with the aim of buying or bartering for food that the farmers raised there, vegetables and poultry. The roads between the city and the villages were infested with German patrols and police dogs. Every suspect caught by these patrols was taken away for investigation. When the Germans caught someone smuggling food they knew well enough they had caught a Jew, for this was their only means of support. The life of the average Pole was hard, but they had access to whatever food supplies were available in the stores.

Every day my family went out to look for food. The first step was to check whether there were any Germans in the vicinity, and this was the job my sister and I had—to serve as lookouts. If we spotted a German, one of us hastened to warn the rest, who would immediately look for a place to hide so that the patrol would not see them. We frequently had to pass by a cemetery. My sister and I were terribly afraid of the dead and always passed it on the run, shivering with fright. We lived thus *for several months, happy every evening because the day had passed safely and we had found some food. On the Sabbath we rested and tried to find hope and encouragement in the news that seeped in from the fronts from the various forbidden sources. But Germany seemed to be making progress in its plan of conquering the world in that year of 1940—Denmark and Norway attacked in April, Belgium and Holland in May. The psychological effect on us was profoundly depressing. Yet we continued to hope, strong in our faith in God, in our conviction that He would not abandon us.*

As the months progressed our present system for smuggling food became increasingly precarious. The German patrols became more numerous and they had a great collection of tricks to catch the unwary in their nets. Many of the inhabitants of Sosnowiec and in the adjoining district of Katowitz were German-speaking and a number of them accepted the German's offer to be classed as Volksdeutsche, meaning German-by-origin, which automatically identified them with the Nazis. Their young joined the Hitlerjugend, the Hitler youth movement, others acted as agents for the Gestapo. Often they were worse than the Germans themselves; cruel, greedy, ready to "sell their brothers for a bowl of porridge" people would say. They were a decided minority amongst the Poles; they had gone to extremes to keep themselves and their families safe. The Germans had further terrorized the public with a "collective" form of punishment: if one member of the family had been caught doing something wrong, the whole family was punished. But they increased the forces against us.

The family held a consultation to discuss what ways and means might be adopted to circumvent the Nazis' watchfulness and keep us alive. They decided that my sister and I, as the least suspect members of the family, must henceforth carry out the whole job and not serve only as lookouts. The idea was to have Maria, our devoted maid, push a baby carriage in which a doll would be placed to look like a baby, with my sister and I walking beside her carrying innocent-looking parcels which would actually contain food, or holding toys whose insides would be filled with foodstuffs. Our problem, however, was that even we children had our enemies, schoolmates who were now among the Volksdeutsche and therefore over-zealous in their attempts to please the invaders. These children, who were taught to hate, began to chase after us, yelling and screaming, "Dirty Jew-girls, what do you have in your parcels? We'll tell the Gestapo right away!"

Once when we did not have the strength left to run, we appealed to a Polish woman and asked for her help against these young toughs. She sent them running with some juicy scolding. Luckily enough, there was no patrol around at the time. We decided that the next day we would go out during school hours to avoid these children.

We continued thus for some months, living in constant fear, in a nightmare that became vivid and terrifying when we would cry out in our sleep, "Run! Hide! A German is coming! The children have seen us!" Mother would wake and hold us, wet with cold sweat, her own eyes streaming with tears, until she succeeded in quieting us and allaying our fears for the moment.

I well remember the day we learned that the German police dogs were trained to sniff our concealed food. The very next day we saw from afar a patrol approaching with a dog. We were near the cemetery at that moment. Quickly, I pulled my sister by the hand and we entered the graveyard through the big iron gate. Running to a distant tomb we put our parcels on the ground and stood shaking from head to toe. As great as our fear of the dead was, we feared the Nazis even more. Not far from us were two women, one weeping over a fresh grave and the other placing flowers on an older tomb. Half an hour we stood there, afraid to breathe, far from the gate, not knowing whether the patrol had passed or was still in the neighbourhood, and terrified to leave lest we fall into their hands. And then came a funeral procession with people streaming into the cemetery, wailing and weeping over the lost dear one. It occurred to me that the best way out was to join the mourners. We crept into the midst of a group of women and thus managed to make our way to safety.

We were not always so successful, even though every day we tried to alter our appearance by wearing something different and combing our hair in a new manner. One day the two of us were caught by a young German, very tall and slim. He was standing on the corner and somehow we failed to notice him in time. When he shouted "Halt! " I looked at my sister and realized my face must be as white as hers. He searched our trembling bodies and found some butter. "So, miserable Jewesses, smuggling, eh? We go to the Gestapo! " We knew that infamous building and the terror it represented. Now we were to go inside.

When we reached it, the soldier left us in the waiting room and went in to his commanding officer.

"I've discovered two smuggling Jewesses," we heard him report proudly.

"Bring them in."

When we entered, we could see that the older officer was taken aback and did not know whether to be angry or amused by the *sight of the two criminals. Two restless dogs were beside him, ready to pounce on us at a word from their master. At last he gave vent to his feelings by rebuking the dogs, with a glint in his eyes:*

"Shut up, both of you! I know you hate Jews; I don't like them any better than you do. But sit still and let me carry on my investigation!"

Turning first to my sister he began to ask her questions and she, frightened out of her wits, stammered incoherently. I hastily explained that she was born deaf and dumb and could not speak. So he fired his questions at me. I repeated the story I had been taught when we embarked on the business of smuggling in our food: my sister and I had been playing outside when a shortish man with brown hair and blue eyes approached us and asked us to deliver this parcel. He would wait on the corner and as a reward give us two bars of chocolate and some candy. We agreed. We did not know this was wrong, and we had not had any sweets for a long time.

"Do you know the man's name?" the officer probed further.

"No, sir, that was the first time we saw him."

He asked me to tell him more about this man. I did not lose my self-control but replied coherently to all his inquiries. Then he asked for our name, and of course I gave him a false name and address, knowing full well that otherwise he would send the black van to take us all to our deaths.

He wrote all the details I gave him carefully in a large book. Then, looking us both over meaningfully, he said gruffly, "Away with you! If I ever catch you again, I'll turn you over to these dogs. They will tear you to pieces!"

Shaking like leaves, we ran home in a long roundabout way, turning frequently to see whether we were being followed. When we got home we did not need to say we had been caught—that was written on our faces. I reported to my parents in full. My sister could not utter a word for days, and we were relieved when she finally regained the power of speech.

Following this terrifying experience we stopped being the family providers, a job we had been fulfilling for an entire year. Again we had the leisure to think and ponder our fate. Instead of living normal lives and going to school like other children our age, we had had to become smugglers, risking our lives and the lives of our whole family in order to eat.

"Why? Why?" I asked repeatedly. And always the answer was the same, "Because you are Jews."

Chapter Thirteen

Each day brought new rumours and whisperings, fresh anxieties. Everyone was always asking questions; no one knew the answers. As it now functioned, Jews aged sixteen to forty had to work for the Germans. The military had depleted the fatherland's labour force, and Jews were cheap and convenient labour, who could be compelled to work long hours, without wages, under constant guard. Many were sent to work camps in Germany, others were kept for the camps in Poland. Some went to the town of Auschwitz, only a half-hour's train ride away, to build the camp there. At first, the name Auschwitz did not raise undue alarm in us—we knew the Jews in the town had been transferred to Sosnowiec, but this was common practice, and we assumed the Nazis were building a maximum security prison for criminals there, albeit a very large one. The place which was to be recorded in history as man's greatest inhumanity to man was in the early months simply another word in our new war-time vocabulary.

In our district there were two SS officers, Knoll and Lindner, responsible for supplying workers for the labour camps, and they both relished the round-ups. Lindner, particularly, enjoyed driving around the streets in a van, catching young Jewish men and women like stray dogs. They were taken to the Dolek, the transit camp, located in a new building that had been originally intended as a secondary school. Then they were shipped off the next day without the chance of telling their families what had happened to them or where they were going. Occasionally letters could be smuggled out and they all told of the same conditions: back-breaking work, long hours, and poor rations. Small wonder our men were soon physically broken, exhausted and spent. The weaker ones fell prey to illness. They were removed—destination unknown—and immediately replaced. The German demands increased and our men and women dreaded the very sight of the Dolek. Finally, when orders came for twenty thousand Jews to be rounded up for the labour camps, the Judenrat, the Jewish Council appointed by the Germans, stepped in.

From the point of view of organization, the Judenrat was one of the great German successes. This institution was established for their own benefit and convenience. It proved to be a most hateful and notorious conception and will long be remembered in our history.

The Judenrat was set up early in the occupation as official representatives of the hundred thousand Jews in Upper Silesia. There was nothing wrong in having representatives, as long as they were chosen by our own people and not by the enemy. And not all of them understood the real intentions of the Germans; they were just puppets, threatened with their own heads if German orders were not carried out. With its headquarters in Sosnowiec and branches in all the towns, the Judenrat consisted of a president, deputies and aides. Assisting them was the Jewish militia, a police force, organized to keep order in the Jewish communities, and direct traffic. This latter was one of the many psychological tricks the Nazis played on us. Certain crossroads and intersections were forbidden to us, and if we approached one of these intersections and wished to continue on, we had to go around the block. And, of course, directing us in this senseless detour were members of the Jewish militia with their white caps and the blue Star of David on their armbands.

The president of the Judenrat was a thirty-eight-year-old man by the name of Merin. He had little education and was a hopeless gambler, but he was nonetheless clever and abounded in self-confidence. His first deputy was a young married woman with a small child, who had been born in Germany and lived there until the age of fifteen. For the higher posts within the Council, Merin selected educated men, well-known in the community; but he gave the most important positions to his own relatives. By means of expensive gifts and bribes he succeeded in establishing friendly relations with Commander Dreier, the German responsible for Jewish affairs in our district, and with the other Gestapo commanders. We had been accustomed to think of Germans as honest people, who kept their promises and never cheated; whose word, we used to say, "is worth more than money". But the war-time German was an altogether different brand, one who stood in full contradiction to all the qualities attributed to his people. This made it possible for Moshe Merin to buy the German's good will and "friendship". Once he discovered that they welcomed his gifts, Merin installed a clerk at a special telephone whose job it was to write down what each of them wished to receive. The telephone rang constantly; the orders came thick and fast; and the fact that the Nazis made some small concessions deluded Merin into thinking that his influence with them was indeed considerable and that he could count on Dreier's promises. As a result he ignored the warnings of educated and experienced men. As time went on, he stopped consulting his associates altogether, for he did not really want to hear the truth. He did not understand that he was only a puppet of the Germans, and that Dreier himself was getting his instructions directly from Berlin and had no authority to make decisions on his own. It is quite possible that Dreier might have hoped to protect his job by protecting the Jews, and avoid being sent to the front—many of his colleagues were not happy at the thought of going into battle—but the final decision was not his to make.

After Lindner had gone to extremes to catch our young people in the streets, the Judenrat offered to undertake the responsibility for supplying the necessary numbers for the camps, expecting thus to be able to prevent their taking married men and the sick who were incapable of withstanding the conditions of the camps. Their intentions were good. The SS officers agreed, on the condition that they would determine the number of men to report each day to the transit camp.

To make it all more official, every Jew was obliged to carry identification bearing a photograph of himself; a copy was kept in the Judenrat offices. The clerks there prepared a card file which facilitated the selection of men for enforced labour and their notification as to the time and place they were to report. Some were rounded up during the night by the Jewish militia. The Judenrat represented Jewish interests, and at the same time it was held responsible for the behaviour of the Jews. Thus the Germans managed to break our unity: the Jewish Council became our most dangerous watchdogs for they knew everyone and everything.

Within a very short time everyone knew of the new function of the Judenrat and that the fate of our young people was in the hands of its president. Suddenly he was the centre of interest, the man in power, and his daughter went about declaring that she was the "daughter of the King of the Jews". In fact the new arrangement, which seemed so helpful to the Jews, proved eventually to be more helpful to the Germans. As time went on, they transmitted all their orders through the Judenrat.

Not all Jews appointed to these Councils were even willing to accept their position—Chernikow, president of the Jewish Council in Warsaw committed suicide rather than carry out German orders. But once the Sosnowiec Judenrat had agreed to select the twenty thousand Jews demanded by the Germans, the militia, who up until now had only been responsible for minor duties, were now assigned to pick up the young men and women who had failed to respond to the written notices. By giving the militia this kind of responsibility, psychologically they became hated symbols among our people. And some of the Jewish militia were not too delicate in performing their duties . . . But all the power that they and Merin and his associates enjoyed was shortlived. They too were included in the extermination plan, and nothing could save them.

We listened secretly to the BBC broadcasts from London, hoping for a sign that the course of events might change. But the news bulletins, published clandestinely by the Polish government-in-exile in London through the Polish underground at home, were depressing throughout the first half of 1941. Victory after victory marked the German war effort. On April 13 the Germans took Belgrade. Later, on the 27th, they entered Athens. In May Rommel's army reached the gates of Palestine and our national home seemed doomed. On June 22, however, the German forces attacked Soviet Russia, and the universal reaction was one of hope. Hitler was following in the steps of Napoleon; he too would be defeated! Salvation seemed possible after all.

But until that time, like it or not, we had to live with our reality of the moment. The Judenrat helped the Germans organize workshops, hoping to increase the productivity of the Jews in Sosnowiec and keep them from being sent away. With the aid of men paid no wages, they produced clothing, shoes, carpen-

try work and the like. Commander Dreier and his aides spread the word that anyone thus employed would be classified as "productive" and "essential", thus ensuring his own and his family's safety. The rest, he explained, were to be transferred to "agricultural settlements", where they would be able to sustain themselves more easily. When the order for the first expulsion arrived, Moshe Merin as president of the Council called a meeting of the Judenrat and the town dignitaries. The question to be considered was whether the Judenrat should co-operate in the act of expulsion and in selecting the first people to be sent away.

"Where are they to be taken?" asked some of those present. "I don't know," was Merin's reply. But instinctively they felt something ominous in the air and decided emphatically not to co-operate as long as they did not know the destination.

"According to the Law," said one pious Jew, "if the enemy demands of a town one man as a hostage, the entire town should go to its death rather than sacrifice that single soul."

"We must be united to the end!" cried another. Each in turn expressed his opinion and the final outcome was a determined "No!"

Then Merin took the floor. "Let us be realistic," he said. "We must see what is best for us here and now and try to save what we can. According to Dreier, if the number named as their quota is expelled, the rest will be allowed to stay." Merin thought he could save the lives of a good number of Jews by trusting in Dreier's promises. If he succeeded in saving even twenty-five per cent of the town's Jews, he reasoned, history would forgive him for selecting the first groups to be expelled.

The decision was his to make, anyway, because behind him stood the German authority, while behind the Jewish populace stood a disorganized people, unarmed, with no alternative. He therefore acted according to his views. The Germans set the quota and the Judenrat sent the notices ordering people to report to a designated location with not more than fifty-five pounds of their personal belongings, such as food for three days, candles, matches, cooking utensils, a basin for washing, etc. Children were to wear name-tags around their necks. However, despite the glowing promises of the agricultural settlements, people had learned to be wary, and very few appeared at the appointed time and place.

But the Nazis were not to be deterred. Since the Jews failed to come of their own free will, the SS arrived early one morning and, surrounding four huge residential buildings, set up shouts of "Everybody out! Come out at once under pain of instant death!" Mothers scarcely had time to put on some clothes and wake their children. The SS officers drove them out with cries of "Quick, quick! Get a move on!" Babies were wailing, little children had to be carried, the old were supported by the younger members of their families. At the head of the frightened procession went the chief rabbi of our town, Rabbi Englender. Turning to look at the people crowded together behind him, he said with self-controlled dignity, "My friends, this is the last road we shall ever travel. But if this is God's will, let us go quietly and in peace, as an example to others. If this is God's will." Calmly he led the way. His presence had a quieting effect on the victims.

They were led into an empty theatre building. Then the young people were taken to the Dolek and from there shipped off to Germany to the various camps. The rest were then packed into a train which took them in the direction of Auschwitz. These were the first Jews to go from Sosnowiec to the death camps of Auschwitz.

Upon returning that evening from the workshops to their homes, many husbands found only empty rooms with here and there a child's toy or a pot still on the stove where a busy housewife had been cooking. They besieged the Judenrat with questions about their loved ones whereabouts. The Council appeased them, saying they had been taken to Theresienstadt, a concentration camp in Czechoslovakia. Postcards began to arrive, announcing—all of them exactly alike—"Arrived safely, feeling well, waiting for you", with an authentic signature to complete the encouraging picture, and relatives at home were persuaded that the missing ones were all right. But when the initial relief faded, suspicions arose—why were all the cards identical? Why did they give no return address?

The second transport was sent off as planned. However, when it was time for the third to leave, the quota fixed by the Germans was not met; the SS therefore broke into orphanages, taking away all the children. Next they invaded old people's homes and dragged the feeble old men and women out and onto trucks. But one hundred more must be supplied. The Nazis surrounded the town's Jewish hospital and rushed in shouting for all the patients to get up at once and line up as they directed. They took patients who couldn't walk, people who had just been operated on and who were writhing in pain. Before leaving, the nurses managed to give some a last shot of pain-killer to relieve their sufferings. Women who had just given birth, even though the placenta was not yet delivered, were forced to walk, blood pouring from them all the way to the trucks. The newborn babies were put in sacks and thrown on the trucks to die before reaching the railway station. Every passerby, Jew or Pole, stopped in their tracks, broke down and wept.

Having seen the evacuation of these young, sick, aged and suffering people, we knew at last that transfer meant one thing—death. For little children and the old or sick are not likely to be taken for resettlement. Where they were taken, how they died, we did not know.

Chapter Fourteen

The first in the series of expulsions triggered a war of nerves, a life-or-death struggle for survival. All our thoughts and actions revolved around the need to avoid being caught, to escape death and remain alive. We were thankful that father had managed to find work in the German food depot, loading foodstuffs and distributing them to various areas of the city. This entitled him to a special certificate confirming that he was an "essential worker". As such he saved our lives. But this did not allay our fears, for, whenever the quota would be short, they might come knocking at our door in the dead of the night and drag off anyone they could find at home.

We no longer dared to spend the nights in our own home. Every night we slept in a different place, at the homes of Polish friends, in deserted cellars or attics, with various people we knew. Children became so inured to danger and reacted so well that their mothers could treat them as adults. One night, when we felt danger in our bones, we shared a shelter with two other families. The group included a child of three. In the middle of the night he awoke and asked for a little milk. "I don't have any, darling," his mother whispered, "but if you cry, the Nazis will come and kill us all."

"Then give me tea," he demanded.

"I have no tea either."

"Then a drink of water," he insisted.

"No, sweetheart, not water or anything else."

The child looked around, forlorn, and then, lying down again, whispered, "But promise me that in the morning you'll give me some water for sure! "

"Of course I will, dear." In a moment he was asleep. It was enough to tell children three or four years old "A German is coming! " to make them scamper away silently and hide.

Each day renewed the problem of where to sleep that night to avoid being caught. Then suddenly my father was struck with an idea: he covered up the door to one room in our apartment with a huge wardrobe so that no one could suspect that such a room even existed.

Father himself had nothing to fear, for he had his essential worker certificate. But he knew that a short quota could mean the end of his family. At night, if we heard footsteps outside, we were afraid to breathe—a knock at the door and I simply froze. One night, when we had gone to bed quite peacefully in our concealed room, I suddenly heard a knock at the outer door and a voice calling, "Open up—Jewish militia." When my father opened the door, he looked so pale and was shaking so hard the policeman asked him whether he was ill. Then they inquired where all the rest of the family was. "They are not home," I heard him reply. "They're spending the night with my in-laws." Next they asked for the whereabouts of a family whose son had failed to report for work in a labour camp in Germany. "That's why we're here," they declared.

I was young, at an age when, normally, girls are just starting to *cast looks of curiosity at the opposite sex, realizing a new relationship with them is imminent. But I was pre-occupied all day, picking up whatever news I could, sifting it, learning ways to avoid danger. Every new movement of the Germans immediately impressed itself on my memory as a precaution. If my social advancement was arrested, my mental and emotional discipline was extraordinarily advanced.*

People were arriving at that period from other parts of Poland with terrifying tales of atrocities the Nazis had perpetrated on children. In a small village not far from Keltz, a company of SS men broke into an orphanage, collected all the children, stuffed them into sacks and buried them alive. Similar savagery was exercised in another village where they let the local Hitlerjugend use Jewish children as shooting targets. Elsewhere they crushed skulls, snatched up people and threw them into trucks bound for unknown destinations.

When reports like these would reach us, the effect was to immediately speed us into action, as if someone were, literally, holding a knife to our throats. We too expected these horrors to descend on us at any moment. It was not surprising, therefore, that after hearing these gruesome stories, our parents' fears mushroomed and they said to my sister and me, "You cannot remain here at home anymore, not another minute. You must go at once to Maria and stay with her until the danger is past." And off we went. Maria had been our refuge so many times.

It was a few days before my parents' fears had eased enough to let us return home. Mother asked us to go outside for a bit of fresh air, "but don't leave the yard." Outside we saw a family friend, whom we were accustomed to seeing well-groomed and dressed, looking quite disheveled and disturbed. This made me suspicious, all the more so when he said that he had something to tell our family and would drop in later. "Is it good news or bad?" I asked, but all he replied was "See you later."

He came in the evening. A number of friends gathered. It was obvious that he was the bearer of deeply distressing news. "What did you hear?" asked my father, without preliminaries.

"Better don't ask!"

"It's better to hear the bitter truth than a sweet lie," father countered.

"Some refugees have come from Wilno," our friend explained. "One woman managed to flee from the Ponar Forest where the Germans dug open ditches, lined the Jews up alongside them, and killed them with machine guns. Their bodies dropped into the ditches. Sometimes mothers and babies are buried alive. It's all been confirmed as true. Men have sneaked into the forests and seen the graves. The woman is not crazy."

For just a moment he paused and then continued, the words stumbling from his mouth. "From Warsaw word has come that a man succeeded in escaping from the Treblinka concentration camp, and he says that in Treblinka the Germans are killing off the Jews with gas and burning their bodies in furnaces!"

"What is happening to our people!" someone shouted.

"They are being taken to Auschwitz and killed in the same way. They are ordered to undress and go into shower rooms, which are really gas chambers, where they meet their death. Their bodies are taken and burned in a crematorium. Some of them are forced to address and sign cards. After they are dead the Germans mail them to us, so we won't become suspicious."

Then he added, "The gas chambers and the furnaces work non-stop, around the clock."

We all sat staring vacantly in front of us. "No, it's not possible," someone cried, "not in our times of civilization and progress! I do not believe it!"

"It is the bitter truth. Let us not delude ourselves any more."

Throughout Poland the news was being reported wherever people met. For most of us it shed a terrifying light on what had been happening. It explained the expulsions, the "resettlements", the trains packed to the roofs, and the postcards which all said the same thing. We knew what Auschwitz was—and it was so close! But some were loathe to believe these stories, especially those who had had personal contacts with the Germans in the pre-war years. It took time to digest this monstrous phenomenon. This attitude characterized the older generation—the young people reacted differently. For them there was only one answer—to organize and rebel, to defend, to fight back. The Germans tried their best to appease through false promises, to weaken unity and offset rebellion. They hinted that it was not their intention to exterminate all Jews, but on the contrary, to establish new labour projects that would offer employment to many more workers, awakening thereby false hopes in many a Jewish heart.

Having heard the news, and realizing what kind of fate awaited me, I began to think very hard. Next morning, responding to a powerful compulsion, I rose early and went for a walk to the railway station, to ascertain that trains bound for Auschwitz did indeed pass through our town. I wandered around the station for hours, watched the passing trains, immediately recognizing the cars in which the victims were huddled. They were easily *identified by the wailing of children begging for water, by the frightened expressions of the women, and by the armed military escort accompanying them.*

After seeing and watching just one such train, I ran all the way home, crying, drank two glasses of water and continued to weep all day long. I could not help myself, I was walking about with tears flowing, unable to say anything about it. "Are you hungry, dear?" mother gently inquired. "No," I replied. "Then why are you crying?" "I'm in a bad mood, that's all," I answered.

At such terrible moments I still consoled myself with the belief that our Polish friend Maria would never let them murder me in cold blood. This reassured me somehow and gave me the courage to go outside again, but always on guard against danger.

I was conscious of one thing above all—that I did not want to die. Whenever I spied a German or a policeman, even at a distance, I changed my direction at once and ran home, my breath heaving. On the other hand, we could not stay locked up in our concealed room forever, for we had to look for food.

Once a month small rations of beans, sugar and jam were distributed according to the number of people in a family and the number of ration cards they possessed. Standing in line for the rations was a risky undertaking; on more than one occasion people did not return from the queue. The Germans had been known to use a cynically cruel ruse: declaring that food was about to be distributed, they would wait until the queue was long enough and then surround it and take everyone away. But we had no alternative, for we were too hungry to relinquish this bit of nourishment. Whenever the notices announcing food dis-

tribution were posted, I would take my sister and together we would hurry in an effort to be first in line. If the store did not open in time, I would instruct my sister to stand in line while I stood watch for any suspicious movements thereabouts. People would be lined up along the whole street. On one such occasion I noticed several people leave their places in line and hurry away. Why, I wondered, and the thought occurred to me that they must have received some inside word, perhaps from a relative serving in the militia, that they had better clear out. I acted fast. Quickly going to my sister and taking her hand, I asked the woman standing in back of her to keep our place because we had to go to the lavatory and would be right back. My alertness and presence of mind were well-timed. A few minutes after we hurried away from the spot, the entire queue was surrounded by armed SS men, and all the people who had been waiting for sugar would never taste it again.

When I saw from my hiding place how they shoved into trucks the young women to whom I had been talking only a minute ago, women who had little children waiting for them at home, I rushed home and burst into sobs. "Mother," I cried, "how long can we go on this way? I am afraid we will be caught in the end. We have so many Polish friends, why don't you arrange that one of them take us in and hide us? Or can't we run away some place where we won't have to see all this and practically smell the smoke from Auschwitz?"

Mother listened in heartbroken misery. "Unfortunately, dear daughter, no. There is no such possibility."

"But why?" I persisted. "Where have all our friends gone? I remember how every Christmas you had trouble dividing up your time because you received so many invitations to their *parties and dinners and dances. Sometimes, in one evening, we would visit many homes to wish them a merry Christmas. And now when we are in such danger . . . you say no . . . ."*

"I considered all those possibilities, darling, some time ago. I went to each of our Polish friends, but I was met with complete indifference, moral and practical. In every home they made me feel unwanted, and I had to leave. Yes, my dear, it seems we did not have real friends. That's why our only hope is God, Who never lets you down. God is just. Human beings are frail, they always disappoint, you can't trust them . . . So don't be afraid. Eat, pray, and go to bed now. I'll look after you as long as I live."

Not yet entirely convinced, I resumed: "Not even our Maria, Mother, not even Maria? Did you ask Maria, Mother?"

Chapter Fifteen

At that moment I was sitting at the table, my head in my hands, remembering when, together with Maria, we had smuggled food home for all of us. Once, as we were making our way back from such an expedition, we tried to reduce the tension we all felt by talking about whatever entered our minds. I had then asked Maria, "Tell me, Maria, how did you first come to our home? And how is it that you've been with us more than ten years?"

"Well," she replied with a smile, "it will sound funny when I tell you that it all started when your mother was big with you." She made a descriptive gesture with her hands, and I laughed. When the time for my birth came, mother went into labour, yet nothing happened. Twenty-four hours passed, the doctor came every few hours, but she made no progress. The doctor finally said, 'If there is no change very soon, then I regret to say I'll have to take the baby with forceps or else perform a Caesarean.'"

"Everyone was worried," Maria said. "Your grandmother went to the cemetery to ask for her mother's intercession on your mother's behalf; she lighted candles, wept and prayed. But there was no change. Your grandfather called his friends together and they prayed for her, and still nothing happened. The doctor meanwhile brought his medical assistants and prepared for the operation. When thirty-six hours of fruitless labour had passed, *he began to boil and sterilize his instruments. Your mother, in the meantime, got such a severe pain that she could not lie still. So, getting out of bed, she walked out of the room on the third floor and down the stairs to the second floor and lay on a bed there. When the doctor had everything ready, he discovered she was not where they had left her. When they brought her up again the delivery began to make quick progress, and very soon you were born, normally and without resorting to surgery."*

"That's all very interesting about me, Maria," I remarked, *"but I still don't know how you happened to come to us."*

"I'll come to that," she assured me, *"if you'll just listen patiently. After your birth, your mother was very weak, and the doctor advised taking in some help so that she could rest as much as she should. It so happened that at the time my mother was working in the same building as a laundress and she offered to bring me to help out."*

"How old were you then?"

"Seventeen. But I was highly experienced by then because for five years I had been taking care of my younger sisters—my mother was away from home all day working. As soon as I came to your house I fell in love with you. You were such a lovely baby, with dark eyes and very fair hair. I had the feeling you were smiling at me and looking at me, even though you couldn't yet see or smile. The minute I entered your home I was overcome by such a good feeling that I accepted the conditions without really listening and began to look after you."

Maria started to laugh as she went on with her story. "I'll never forget the funny experiences I had. Once when I took you for a walk in my own neighbourhood, I met a girlfriend. She looked at you and then at me and then cried, 'Maria, I always thought we were good friends; we never quarreled; we got along well, so I don't see why you didn't invite me to your wedding! You've already got a daughter and I didn't even know!' "

"I burst out laughing and said, 'Christina, I promise you, when I decide to get married, you'll be one of the first to be invited to the wedding!' "

" 'And this child, you mean to say she is not yours?' she asked. She couldn't believe it."

" 'No,' I told her, 'she isn't my child.' "

" 'But she looks so much like you!' she said in amazement."

"Another day I met another friend, and she also rebuked me as Christina had. 'Who is the prince on a white horse who made you forget to invite your friends to the wedding?' And she added, 'It's not that I'm angry, just curious.' When I told her I was still waiting for my prince to appear and that you were not my daughter, she could hardly believe it."

"And then—you can't imagine how excited I was—I met a boy and fell madly in love with him, but I didn't know how he felt about me. One day he saw me walking with you, and he stopped and turned white as a sheet. And then he put on an act. Congratulating me in a sarcastic tone, he said, 'It's interesting Maria: whenever I wanted to see you, you put me off with one excuse or another—either you were too young to go out, or your mother wouldn't allow it, or you were too busy looking after your sisters. I'm sure you know I love you and want very much to be with you. Yet you never had time for me, but you had time for someone else, I can see that now—you have a child to prove it.' "

"I can tell you that was the happiest moment of my life. It was the first declaration of love anyone had ever made to me, and it was clear to me that it was genuine. So now I knew our feelings were mutual. I said to him, 'If I was not free to go out with you, I was certainly not free to go out with other boys.' "

"His eyes began to sparkle. 'You mean this is not your own child?' "

" 'No, she is not my child,' I replied, and he caught me to him, kissing and hugging me joyously . . . And of course it was him I married," Maria concluded, "but not right away since we were both too young. After this meeting I was very happy, and I took tender care of you. I used to bathe you, feed you, play with you and take you for walks. Your whole little world circled around me."

Many other questions were on the tip of my tongue, but as we reached home just then, we decided to talk more about the subject the next day.

When we resumed again, Maria told me about her childhood. Her father, a miner, had died in a mine explosion when she was about my age, and she had to leave school and stay home to take care of the younger children so her mother could earn a livelihood. By the time Maria began to work for us, the other children were old enough to look after themselves. And she had been with us ever since.

"Didn't you ever think you could get a better place to work than in our house?" I asked her.

"Only once, and that was because they promised better wages," she answered. *"One day a neighbour who lived across the way offered to pay me much more to work for her. I myself wasn't eager to accept the offer, but I made the mistake of mentioning it to my mother, and she kept insisting that, after all, it's only a job—I should take advantage of a chance to earn more money. She didn't understand that there are things more important than money."*

"What, for instance, Maria?"

"Well, she didn't appreciate the fact that at your house I had found something I lacked at home."

"Such as what?"

"Well, my mother was a middle-aged woman who worked very hard every day as a laundress. When she got home she was so worn out she never had any strength or patience for us children. She used to scold and shout at us and insist that we leave her alone and let her get some rest. She herself demanded understanding and consideration and yet she didn't seem to realize that she gave us none, even though we, as children, needed it too."

"When I came to work at your house and was given attention, and courtesy and consideration even in small things, my heart overflowed with gratitude. Only then did I see how much I needed and missed these qualities in my life. Whenever I was in a bad mood, for example, your mother would say, 'Now, Maria, don't you worry. You're a good-looking girl, with a nice figure and lovely hair and eyes. I'm only afraid that one fine day a prince charming will come and snatch you away from us.' Until then no one ever told me I was attractive. It was so

encouraging for me; it lifted my spirits and buoyed me up. Your mother used to go with me to buy clothes and guide me so that I'd be well-groomed and look nice. And on all kinds of occasions she would buy me a present. Perhaps someone who was not as starved for affection as I was wouldn't have appreciated these things as deeply as I did."

"But for my mother, more pay was the main thing. She pressed me so hard I finally said I would take the other job. When I told your mother, she was completely bewildered. 'Why are you leaving us suddenly? We've never had a quarrel; you've never complained of anything. So what is the reason?' I told her it was the money. 'In that case, go in peace and good luck to you! I'm glad that's the only reason,' she said. I packed my things, said goodbye and left. You were two years old at the time, and I loved you with all my heart...."

"A few days later you became sick. You had a high temperature and you stopped eating altogether. The doctor was mystified; he could not diagnose your illness. He came every day but to no avail. None of the medicines he tried helped. Your condition finally became very serious. When I heard about it, I came and stood at your window for hours, crying my heart out, but I was ashamed to go in. On Sunday I got up very early, went to church, fell on my knees before the Holy Cross and wept and prayed for your health and for the chance to go back to work at your house."

"When I learned that you were getting worse and that they were thinking of taking you to the hospital, I was beside myself with worry. So I rushed to the priest and asked for confession. 'Tell me what is in your heart,' the priest urged. I told him everything and asked whether I had committed a sin by leaving you. 'No,' he assured me, 'it is not a sin to want to improve your *work conditions and salary.'* "

" '*But I'm so miserable,*' *I wept,* '*I don't like the new place or the children. I want to go back!* ' "

" '*In that case I suggest you go and visit the sick child, and if they ask you to stay, then stay with them.*' "

"As soon as I opened the door to your room, you leapt out of bed and began to hug and kiss me. In no time your temperature was down to normal. You asked me to feed you. Everyone was overjoyed. And I swore to Jesus Christ that I'd never leave you again until I'd married and had children of my own."

When she finished, I had just one more question. "Maria, tell me this: how did you feel working in a Jewish home?"

"I was very happy," she cried enthusiastically. "I learned to respect other religions, mostly because I saw what respect your whole family showed for my religion. In winter, when it was bitter cold and snowing, I used to sleep at your house. But in the morning your mother would wake me up and say, 'Maria, it's late, you have to get up and go to church.' It puzzled me that she should be so concerned that I observe my religion, and one day I asked her about this. I'll never forget her answer. 'Maria,' she told me, 'everyone is born into a tradition to which he belongs. I was born Jewish and shall go on being Jewish always. You were born Christian and it is your duty to go on being a good Christian. We are all children of one God, and there will always be love among us if we respect each other's faith. God wants us all to be decent and honest, to seek justice and truth. If you stick to this, I'll never be afraid to leave my children in your care.' "

"When you were six years old I asked permission to take you to church one Sunday morning. When we came out again, you asked me, 'Maria, we have our God and you have your God—how many more are there?' I always laughed recalling that one!"

So, this was our Maria, whom I loved so much, and who, I was certain beyond the shadow of a doubt, would never disappoint me. She was my hope and my consolation in the darkest hours. That is why I asked mother, "Not even Maria?"

"No," answered mother. "Oh, Maria would be ready to help us."

"So what is the problem?" I insisted.

"Listen and I'll tell you," my mother said, looking distressed. "It was the last time we were at Maria's, you remember, it wasn't too long ago. In the morning the two of you were still asleep, but father and I were awake and anxiously waiting for news. There was a knock at the door. A delegation of women from the village entered. I listened behind the door, because I had a premonition of trouble. 'We represent all the neighbours, Maria,' one of them declared sternly, 'and we've come to warn you. We know you are hiding Jews in your house. You must send them away at once. This time it is only a warning, but if you should hide Jews ever again, we will inform the Gestapo and you know what to expect from them . . . .' "

"Maria stood pale and silent. When they left, I came into the room and found her crying. I said, 'I heard what she said. We will leave right away.' She hid her face in her hands. 'I am ashamed as a human being,' she sobbed, 'and as a Christian. Those women have forgotten Christ's teachings. And they've *forgotten that we all have a common enemy.'* "

"I told her that we appreciated her wanting to help us. 'I'm glad to know there are Poles like you who are ready to share what little they have with others in a time of need. It's good to know this, but we cannot put you in danger anymore. You are a wife and the mother of two little children. You will all be in grave peril if we stay. It is possible to guard against an enemy from without, but hardly possible to guard against your own people.' "

"So you see, dear, Maria cannot help us either."

I nodded my head very quietly.

Chapter Sixteen

We had abandoned the idea of the secret room in our own home and were once again sleeping in whatever cellars and rooms we could find which looked like they would be safe for the moment. Finally, the inevitable happened. Early one morning news reached us that all Jews who had stayed the night in their homes on our street had been taken away and the street declared Judenrein. Wearily and fearfully, we stole into our home. It had been emptied of everything it contained by our Polish neighbours; they even took our family pictures. All that was left to us were the clothes on our backs. We looked around the house in which we had lived for so long, that held so many memories for each of us, and stealthily as thieves, we then left, careful not to be noticed by any of the neighbours. So we took our leave of the past and crept to the centre of town, to the office of the Judenrat's welfare bureau, and presented ourselves to the officers who attended to refugees who had nothing left. The Judenrat would take over property left by Jews transported to Auschwitz and distribute it among the needy. The officer gave us an abandoned flat, two beds, a table, some blankets and pillows, a few kitchen utensils, some clothes and a little money. We settled down in our new home and tried to live as normally as we could.

But I could find no peace. I could not reconcile myself to the hostility that Maria's neighbours had shown toward us, even though they did not know us personally; or to the greediness of our own neighbours. Why did they have no sympathy for our plight? Why would they rather have the Germans exterminate us like rats? Why? WHY? I remembered an episode that occurred shortly before the third transport to Auschwitz left our town. I was in bed, supposedly asleep. One of our Polish neighbour-women came in and, clearing her throat in embarrassment, I heard her say to my mother, mumbling and stammering, "You know . . . I was sent by the rest of the neighbours . . . It's rather embarrassing for me . . . But you know what is ahead of you . . . Sooner or later they will kill you all . . . And they'll take everything away . . . Why give the Nazis your property? Better give it to your neighbours, distribute it among us . . . ."

My parents cut her short. "We have not yet decided how to divide the inheritance," they told her. "When we do, we'll let you know."

When she left the house, I could hear mother telling father, with painful irony, "The Germans knew where to build their extermination machine. They knew that here the people would care more for some miserable furniture than for a human life. They're like beasts of prey, lying in wait, ready to pounce . . . ."

"Mother," I asked her next morning, "do all the Poles act this way?"

"No, dear," she replied quickly, "there are many mean types, but there are others—we cannot know how many, but they do exist—who are gentle and noble, fair-minded people who feel respect for other human beings and who risk their lives to try to help others. These people put themselves in a very precarious position. They take twice the risk and should be twice blessed. They have so many enemies, the Germans and their Polish brothers. It is our bad luck that we do not count such souls among the Poles we thought were our friends...."

"Why is it we don't have neighbours like that?" I asked.

Mother reflected for a moment, then answered me slowly, as if picking her way through her own thoughts. "I can only give you a general reason ... but it seems to me it's true. In the larger centres where there are more educated people, it is different. The Germans found it more difficult to buy them off with propaganda. Then, too, many of those Poles feel no hostility towards the Jews. They are more objective, more humane, more conscious of the fact that we all have the same enemy. The Polish underground also takes a different attitude. But here there is no underground, and the majority are far from educated and enlightened. Most of them are sharecroppers, miners, labourers, and have been for many generations. Their life must seem very hopeless to them most of the time. The Germans give them the dream of a better life if the Jews disappear, and they are easy targets for the propaganda machine. The few like our Maria cannot fight the majority." She concluded with a deep sigh, "Our only hope is in God Almighty. He will not abandon us."

There was indeed no other hope; even my child's mind grasped that fact clearly enough. It was comforting in those days of profound despair to sense that the Divine Presence was watching over us to keep us safe. There were very few families intact in 1942 and I could take comfort, too, in the fact that we were all still together.

The abnormal conditions under which we lived and which were now an integral part of our lives created a new kind of human being. Gradually one became less sensitive, less compassionate, *more and more lethargic and indifferent. The letters from the Jewish young people in the labour camps of Germany, which had upset us so much in the early months, did not seem so distressing now. At least they were alive and not in the gas chambers. The loss of relatives became a matter of routine, to be accepted with apathy. I witnessed with my own eyes many a scene of sons returning home to find none of their loved ones left. In the early days people wept, screamed, rent their hair; but in time they became indifferent. The new being who evolved was egocentric, determined to live, to survive. That was all he thought or cared about. The fear of the unknown got hold of us, the fear of sudden death. The temporarily saved was glad he was saved, not knowing if the next day he would be among the "quick". Yet everyone hoped for tomorrow's miracle, a complete change in the situation. This irrational hope, combined with a belief that the world's conscience would be aroused, gave people the strength to struggle on . . . .*

Chapter Seventeen

July 1942. A hot summer day. Everything was blossoming and flowering. The air was full of gaiety. Even for us the sun was shining. The wonderful weather had its effect—I dressed and crossed the bridge to the other side of town, where I could see boys and girls my own age quibbling, all in a free and lighthearted manner. How I envied them! They live in a different world, I thought to myself, a lovely world without fear or worry. Seeing them walking along with their schoolbags on their backs, an expression of peace and contentment on their faces, waving goodbye to their mothers, I imagined myself doing the same—and broke into sudden tears. I recalled the bell ringing and all of us lining up for class. My thoughts entered into another plane, like a dream. "If I had the chance," I thought, "I'd be a good student. I like to study. I've known since the first memory of my own thoughts that education would open up everything for me." And my mind moved on again. "Who are the guilty ones? Why can't I be like other children? Why am I different? Somebody must have made a mistake somewhere in the past. I can't solve these questions, but whoever was responsible, I hate them. They did not see into the future, they only saw the present." And there followed minutes when my heart was so filled with hate I couldn't express it, even to myself. Somehow, somewhere, something went wrong. Somehow, on this side of the bridge I shake with the fear of being killed, and on the other side my school friends have the joy of life. Myself, and others like me, do not even have the right to live. I was sure at that moment there were people who were responsible for allowing this to happen, people you could point your finger at and say, "I accuse you." And I did, with a full and heavy heart.

There wasn't much time to ponder and think abstractly, however. I came back to reality and headed to the centre of town. I was once again surrounded by wretchedly unhappy children like myself. Yet, despite this, I could detect an unusual sense of excitement; an air of gaiety absent since the beginning of the war. It was not just the weather, no—the smiles of men and women in the street indicated something more meaningful. Watching carefully, I could hear the comments people were making as they met. "Have you heard?" "Did you hear the latest news?" I decided to find out what it was and, if it was good, I'd hurry home to my parents with it.

There was no difficulty in finding out. Our people had been in constant contact with the Polish underground, who in turn were in contact with the Polish government-in-exile in London, led by General Sikorsky. The news that our people found so encouraging that bright July day was that, for the first time, Sikorsky, speaking on the BBC, had informed his world-wide audience of the fact that Jews were being systematically liquidated in the camps of Auschwitz, Treblinka, and others. Now the whole world knew; rescue would not be long in coming. The nations of the world would not tolerate the slaughter.

Speculation ran wild. Many assumed that the first act on the part of the Allies would be to bomb the gas chambers and crematoria. "Now, don't worry," they consoled one another, "the end is near." "One of these mornings we'll wake up and hear that English planes bombed Auschwitz, Belsetz, Maidanek, Treblinka . . ." "And don't forget that there are many Germans in America and England. Hitler will be made to realize that his cruelty will work against him. He'll have to change his tune!" "Now, stop whining, keep hope, heads up!"

That was the mood and it proved infectious. Now we listened night after night for the sound of the anticipated explosions... But nothing happened. Still, we did not give up. We thought, if not tonight, perhaps tomorrow. There'll be more than enough Jewish volunteers to aid from the ground, if only the order will be given to bomb. But there was only silence, and the smoke continued to pour from the crematoria.

We were still in a hopeful state of mind when, later in the month, the president of the Judenrat assembled us and announced that on August 12 we would all have to report to the sports grounds to have our certificates stamped by the Gestapo officials. A series of propaganda meetings was conducted by the Judenrat in an effort to create a festive mood for the day. But with three years' experience behind us, we all felt skeptical and wondered endlessly what the Germans really had in mind and whether or not to report. There were twenty-one thousand Jews at that time in Sosnowiec. Counting both the town and surroundings, about fifty thousand Jews were expected to report on the appointed day. Common sense said they could not take fifty thousand and kill them all in a single day, or even transfer them all to an extermination camp, for they would be unable to absorb us all. And yet....

On the other hand, how could Father, classified as an essential worker, go to work without having his certificate stamped? There was our answer—we had to go.

The day was fast approaching. Before finally making up our minds, we went to visit a friend of the family, an auditor em-

ployed by the Judenrat. He received us cordially and after discussing all the pros and cons of the situation, we asked him: "Will you and your family report?" He assured us they would.

Thus it happened that we were among the twenty-one thousand Jews who reported to the sports stadium in August, 1942, naively thinking they were just to have their certificates stamped. The first to report that morning were the president of the Judenrat, Moshe Merin, his wife, daughter and parents, followed by all their employees. Their example exerted a tremendous impact. All the rest followed their lead, thousands upon thousands—except for the very sick, who were exempted—with their food baskets in their hands.

The day was very hot. Mother dressed herself and us in light summer dresses, our Sabbath best. Father also wore his Sabbath suit. We packed a small basket of food and went off as though bound for a picnic.

At noon the gates were closed and armed guards were posted. No one was permitted to leave. The huge stadium was full.

I shall never forget the twenty-four hours in that stadium. Hours passed, but no one was allowed to leave, no announcements were made. Rumours began to make the rounds that machine guns were being installed all around the stadium.

Shortly before sunset it began to rain. The sky was dark and threatening. Panic spread like wildfire. Children, tired and hungry, set up a weeping and wailing; mothers scampered about in a frenzy helplessly holding their tots in their arms, not knowing how to calm them. The lightly dressed people were now shaking with grief and cold. Some cried, others became hysterical, but most were silent, numbly awaiting the next development.

In the evening we were ordered to line up, eight in a row. Tables were brought in and high-ranking Nazi officers took their places behind them. Each family in turn was directed to step forward, and they made a selection by calling out a number. "One" meant that you were free to leave, "two" that you were to go to a forced labour camp, "three" that you could appeal, and "four" meant assignment to a transport.

We realized then that we had fallen like animals into a trap, but it was too late to regret our naivete and foolishness. Merin's propaganda, the influence of the broadcasts, and the fear of remaining without a stamped certificate had blinded us to reality.

We were soaked to the skin, trembling with cold, thirsty, hungry, worn out. But we stood quietly and tried to keep ourselves calm. When we became too tired, my sister and I sat down on the wet muddy grass in our light summer clothes. Our parents wished to be last in line in the hope that by winning time they would somehow also win our freedom. It was the longest night of my life. There was so much water—the rain poured down. Standing was difficult and sitting became impossible, and one cannot describe how we looked. Within a few hours we had changed so much it would have been impossible to recognize us. What fatigue and fear had not accomplished, the pouring rain had. To keep myself occupied I wandered about the crowd and listened to the talk of the people. Even the rain aroused different opinions. Some said that God was crying for us. Others declared ours was a sinful generation and that the few righteous souls in our midst could not save the many, many sinners; all would be punished. And still others cried out that they could no longer believe in God, for if He could see the pain and suffering and do nothing about it, they could no longer put their faith in Him.

The ones who suffered most that night were the little children. Any appeal for help or consideration for them was met with laughter and derision. I could not believe that, when confronted face to face with Jewish children, the Nazis could take such sadistic pleasure in tormenting them. None of their bestial crimes was as great as their inhuman treatment of little ones. At that moment I was glad my parents did not have a baby to worry about.

Time crawled. The Nazi officers became tired and hungry and, leaving the tables, went out to eat and rest. During the hours they were gone we were forced to wait. When the first signs of dawn appeared we were still standing, still hoping for salvation. Early in the morning they returned. We approached the table. The Nazi officer examined us and then our certificate and then barked one word to seal our fate: "Three! " The guards moved us at once to group three. We were caught in the death net. There was no going out to freedom for us, only the possibility of an appeal that would certainly be ignored or rejected.

How can one describe the sensation of being doomed, of being sentenced to death without a trial, for no explicable reason, for no crime committed?

Some became hysterical, others were completely indifferent. Many lost their minds in that twenty-four hours. The ones whom I had heard crying "There is no God! " were the ones who started to scream. It is too much for the human mind to be disappointed in everything at once—in human beings and in God—and their minds snapped. Those who could at least hold on to their faith in God were able to keep going with courage. I could only envy the very small children who did not under-

stand what was happening.

Later that morning we were ordered to line up in rows of ten. About ten thousand had been assigned to transports, but only a part of that group was taken straight to the railroad station and shipped off to Auschwitz. As there was simply not enough room in Auschwitz to absorb in one day the ten thousand people from our town in addition to the many thousands arriving from all over Europe, the rest of them were transferred to buildings in streets that had previously been emptied of all their occupants. Under heavy guard we were marched from the stadium to Four Targowa Street. There we were to wait until the call came from Auschwitz that there was room for us.

As we were marching, my mother gave my sister a sign to run away. She slipped out of line without the guards noticing. Mother then made a sign to me, but I was afraid of endangering her by trying to escape and being caught. I stayed in line, and later it was impossible to leave.

We were led into a huge building and dispersed amongst the rooms. The gate was locked behind us, with two SS guards posted on either side. Only the Jewish militia and members of the Judenrat were allowed to come and go.

I drank some water straight from the faucet, washed my hands and face, and went to sleep. But the noise was so great that after only two hours I awoke. I went out to the balcony where I could view one of our main thoroughfares, Morzjowska Street. Masses of relatives were gathered, crying and waving, while our people were crowding at the windows and on the balconies shouting, "Help! Help!" as if there was anyone around who could help . . . . I stepped back in and wandered about the rooms, observing my fellow Jews. In one room I saw a young woman with big black eyes sitting on the floor holding a bundle of rags bound together in the form of a baby, singing it a lullaby, "Sleep, my baby, sleep...." Watching her for a minute was more than I could bear and I moved to the next room. Here I saw something I thought I would never see: people were sitting on the floor mourning their own deaths, looking like real corpses, only capable of feeling pain. I left and went to a third room. A young and beautiful woman leaped toward me, crying, embracing me and kissing me in a frenzy of joy, murmuring all the time, "Rosele, Rosele, my darling, my love, my beloved daughter, I've been searching for you—thank God I've found you!" I stared at her, puzzled. "My name is not Rosele and I am not your daughter," I objected.

"Yes, you are, you are my Rosele," she insisted, her voice becoming shrill. "Don't you recognize your own mother, darling?"

"No," I cried, thoroughly upset, "you are not my mother! My mother is in the next room!" I turned and ran into our room. But she was right behind me, arms outstretched to seize me. Taking hold of my mother, I shouted, "You see, this is my mother!" Mother sized up the situation at once, realizing that the poor woman had lost her mind after her husband and daughter were taken from her and put on the morning train. Putting her arm around the weeping woman's shoulder, she tried to calm her down as she led her gently away. I stayed in our room after that, afraid to leave my mother for a minute.

Every now and then one of the militia men would come in, call out a name, and release the person. Those were the people who were able to pay large sums of money or turn over valuable jewelry in return for their release. The German guards were easy to bribe. But we had nothing to offer. Then our auditor friend came in looking for someone. Although penniless, my mother hurried over to him. "Mr. Doron," she greeted him, "you see we too are here. But I'll give you what we have, even though it isn't much—here, take my ring—only save my daughter!" And taking off her wedding ring, she offered it to him. But he only stared and said coldly, "Who are you, Madame? I don't know you. Leave me alone."

Pale as a ghost, my mother cried, "Oh, Mr. Doron, have I changed so much this last day that you don't recognize me?"

"I don't know you, and I never knew you." He tried to pass her by. "Now let me find the person I'm looking for."

She started crying. Since that moment, I stopped believing in human beings. I no longer believed in their good intentions, realizing that humans can be turned into real beasts.

In the evening food was brought in huge pots, but it was gone so quickly we did not get a chance to taste it. The empty vessels were used to smuggle little children out to freedom. I was not one of them, however, for these were deals set up by members of the Jewish police to save their relatives and no one in our very large family had agreed to serve in the militia.

I had no desire to eat, but I did want a drink. The day was Friday. I remember this because, as I was looking in the cupboard for a glass, I found some candlesticks and candles, the mute remains of some family's life in these rooms. Taking them to my mother, I saw she was very happy to be able to bless the Sabbath candles once again on this Friday evening. After lighting the candles she voiced a simple prayer in a firm, quiet voice: "God in heaven, perhaps I was not virtuous enough, but I observed the laws of the Book. Help me to save my children.

115

Listen to my prayer, You are my only hope. Only in You do I believe. Men are cruel and disappointing and only You are just. Please, please God, don't take my children's souls when they are still so very young," and she burst into heartbroken sobs, the hot tears running down her thin cheeks. I wept with her and then, sipping some cold water, went wearily to sleep. I knew that tomorrow at this time I would no longer be alive. I thought, "What is there left for me to do?" As I shut my eyes, I said a prayer in my own words: "My Lord, I don't know if I have obeyed all the laws, but I tried to be a good Jew. I want to live—I don't want to die, but if I have to, please take me in my sleep. Let me sleep forever and ever. Please, I am so afraid of standing in line tomorrow to be gassed and burned . . . ." I did not know then that my father, along with three other men, was planning an escape for that very night.

We were three families in the room, including an aged couple whose son was a policeman. It was he who had suggested the escape. He said he would wait below in the street, under our window, and would signal us when to climb down out of the window with the help of a rope. But he laid down one condition—that his mother would be the first. His plan was accepted with alacrity.

There was no rope, but the men tied together some bed sheets, planning the operation for two o'clock in the morning. At one o'clock those sleeping were awakened and told of the plan. Just past two o'clock the policeman gave the sign and his mother began to climb down as had been agreed. As she approached the street level, he held her feet and brought her down gently to avoid making the slightest sound. The first person had succeeded: she was saved. Next came my turn. I kissed my mother and father, took hold of the sheet and descended it swiftly. But as I started to run down the street, a German patrol emerged, *noticed me and shouted, "Halt!" as they began to give chase. I did not stop. They shot volley after volley in my direction, as if I was the biggest criminal in the world, but I ran on. In back of the building were the cellars. I leapt into one of them and the Nazis charged past, missing me altogether. I heard them running and shouting, but they did not find me. I huddled against the wall, my heart beating wildly.*

After a while silence fell. I was standing in the cellar all alone. In the pale light filtering in, I could see mice and rats, first only a few and then whole groups of them. I was terrified of them. Whom I feared more, the beasts on two legs or those on four there in the dank cellar, it is hard to say. The rats were as big as cats and they rushed about, often on my feet and legs. I felt I had to explain my desperate situation to them and I carried on a silent appeal to them in my mind. "Please, please leave me in peace. Everything is against me. You, at least, please leave me alone." It was still night, and until six in the morning a Jew was not permitted on the street. Outside were Nazi patrols. But only four houses away lived some acquaintances of ours—should I take the risk and try to sneak over there?

Terrified of the horrid creatures all around me, I was tempted to run for it, no matter what. As I was weighing this possibility, I suddenly heard a loud thump, like two bodies colliding, followed by running footsteps and then the siren of an approaching ambulance. I did not know what had happened, who had succeeded in escaping and who had failed. I knew that it was a question of life and death and everybody would do their best. A woman in the group had been scheduled to climb down after me. Had she done so? I peeped out and noticed that as the ambulance drove away the SS officers installed powerful projectors to light the whole area. I had to stay where I was.

117

In the morning I found the courage to look out and then jumped out quickly, passed the dangerous piece of sidewalk and in a moment found myself mingling with the temporarily free. I went home, and there was my sister. She leapt up joyously on seeing me and ran to hug me. "Where are mummy and daddy?" she asked. I told her what had happened and changed my clothes. My sister insisted I must rest a while.

At noon we went to the street where the arrested Jews were being held. I looked toward the window and balcony of our room but could not see or hear anything. We stood and searched among the crowd, hoping to see someone we knew. Suddenly I saw mother's younger sister, who had come for the same purpose. She was just as happy to find us, and we were talking over what we ought to do next when a man I did not know approached us and asked to speak to my aunt alone. They went off to one side. A few minutes later she turned back to us, so pale and distressed that we were frightened.

"What's happened? Were they taken to the railway station?" we both asked in terror.

To this she did not reply. "Come," she urged us gently. "There's no use standing here, let's go home. You must eat something."

I had a premonition of disaster but was too exhausted to probe further. I let myself be shepherded home. A few hours later father came in. As a holder of an essential worker certificate, he had been released in the morning.

"Where's mother?" we cried out.

"In the hospital," he answered.

"But why? How is she?"

"Don't ask me now, I'm too confused," he begged.

"Then let's go and see her," we insisted.

At the entrance to the hospital we met another aunt. Her two sons lay in the epidemological department, both stricken with typhus. Her husband had been sent off to a labour camp in Germany. She herself, being the holder of an essential worker certificate, had been released. At once she hurried to the hospital to look after her sons. When she heard the ambulance she went to see who had been brought in—and recognized her sister. Now her eyes were red and swollen.

"Aunt Regina," we cried, *"what's the matter?"*

"There is no change," she told us.

We went up to the surgical department. The silence in the corridor made us shiver. A nurse asked whom we wanted to see, and when we told her she took us to room 250. As we tiptoed in, we thought mother must be asleep.

"Mother," I said softly—I felt I had to speak softly—*"Why don't you speak to us?"*

Her eyes fluttered open and immediately closed again. *"Why does she have all that ice on her head,"* I wondered. I did not know she was unconscious because she had fractured her skull.

"Your mother is unconscious," the nurse said, *"but you may go on talking to her; I see she reacts well to your presence."*

We stood there dumbfounded. Then my sister crept up to her and begged, "Mummy darling, get well soon and come home. It's so sad without you. We love you. I can't eat or sleep when you're not there. Come back soon, Mummy."

Again her eyes fluttered. There was an oppressive silence in the room, but we stayed quietly beside her. Late in the afternoon the nurse came hurrying in and whispered to father that we must not stay any longer. There was word that the hospital might be surrounded and everyone taken away. We did not want to go, but she ordered us out.

"Come back tomorrow," she said, in an effort to persuade us. Father, his certificate in hand, was allowed to remain.

There was only silence and sadness at home. We lay down in our clothes, not speaking a word. Early in the morning father returned. We scarcely recognized him. I stared at him, afraid to ask questions.

"Go back to sleep," he said hoarsely. "I'll be right back."

It was to make the funeral arrangements that he went. A few hours later he came back. Gently he told us. "Now get dressed," he directed us. "We must go. The funeral will be in the new cemetery."

We were six persons altogether. The gravedigger was the one who conducted the burial service. After it was over he addressed a few words to us personally. "There is nothing I can say to console you in your great loss," the simple soul said in his sincerity, "except that in the forty years I have worked as a gravedigger, I have never buried such a beautiful woman. May you never know sorrow again."

We left. The tears flowed freely for hours and then we sank into complete apathy and despair, indifferent to the dangers lying ahead.

We recovered slowly from the shock and stupor of mother's death and began to adjust to living without her. But one thing gave us no peace—the need to know what had happened the night I escaped, what had caused her death. To avoid hurting father, we postponed the question until one day when, apropos of another matter, it came up naturally.

It was right after I had slid down the rope, making my escape. When they heard the SS men chasing me, shooting as they ran, there was no way of knowing whether I was safe or hurt or dead. Overwrought by all this, mother had insisted that she must climb down immediately because I might need her help. She had to find out what had happened to me. The others, seeing her state of mind, let her climb down out of turn. Without a word they let her down to the street. But as she was nearing the pavement, frightened perhaps when she felt the Jewish policeman's hands on her feet to prevent her making a sound, she let go and fell to the ground, striking her head on an iron ring that lay nearby. It was this that caused the fatal concussion, the heavy thump I had heard while hidden in the cellar. No one else was able to escape that night.

We were not the only ones in our building to lose a member of the family; there was not a family that had not lost mother, father or both. Everyone was in mourning. A few days later, when my sister and I had not been seen outside at all—father was off at work all day, of course—a neighbour from the floor above came to look for us. Finding us in tears, she cried, "You are very wrong to take it this way!" I wondered why she had come in—just to tell us to behave properly? "Stop crying and just realize how lucky your mother was. She was a good woman and she at least had her reward, for she was one of the very few to be buried properly according to all the rules of our tradition, and not queue up for the gas chamber in a Nazi concentration camp as the rest of us are bound to do. It is only a matter of time . . . . You weep and weep when you should be glad, because you loved your mother. For us there is no chance, no one will try to save us, no one who could help is willing to do anything for us.'"

"What do you mean?" I asked, for I sensed that she was referring to something specific.

"Now I can tell you," she replied, "because they are no more. My daughter and her children appealed to a nunnery for refuge but they were turned away by the nuns, who said they had no room in their nunnery for Jews and would not endanger anyone for their sakes . . ." She wiped her eyes and went on. "They even lectured her to accept her fate because it was God's will. 'You are to be destroyed and must accept it with love,' that's what they told her. So she went to other nunneries but they all refused. Some were polite and others didn't even bother to be polite . . . ."

I saw before me a bitter, broken woman who consoled herself with the conviction that we would all end up in the same horrible way as her nearest and dearest had done. She may have been right, I thought, but it was hard to accept. She was, as a matter of fact, not alone in her opinion; others too tried to console us with similar arguments, even expressing outright envy at my mother's great good fortune.

But we were young, and our instincts made us feel that while there was life in us we must try to go on living and hoping, *even though at the moment our chances for survival seemed non-existent. I wept so much during this time that for the next twenty years, even in the most distressing situations, I could not shed a tear.*

Time passed, and we realized we were unable to change reality, but would have to reconcile ourselves to it. Forced to take courage and seek for a new source of strength, we opened the door and set out to look for contact with the world outside.

Chapter Eighteen

"Good morning, children!" This friendly greeting came from Mania, our twenty-year-old neighbour. "How are you doing?"

"We're still alive," I answered, "though not much more than that. Who is missing in your family?"

That was the way we conversed in those days. She answered with the same directness. "Everybody. Only a cousin of mine and I are still here."

"I'm sorry to hear that. We hardly know your cousin."

"He arrived not long ago with his parents after they escaped from a village near Cracow that was declared Judenrein. We took them in, got them a permit to stay, and even got a job for Jacob."

"Out of the frying pan into the fire," was my retort.

"Yes," she sighed, "what a terrible time to live in."

Our common fate drew us close to each other. It was still summer and our doors were open most of the time. In the morning Mania and Jacob hurried off to work, she in a clothing workshop and he in a carpentry shop. We always waited to see them pass our door. The minute I heard their footsteps early in the *morning, I rushed to the door to say hello. I always had questions to ask, for, being two years older than my sister and having been suddenly catapulted into replacing my mother as lady of the house, quite without preparation, I needed help every day. Mania was very patient and explained carefully what I wanted to know about cooking, laundry and the rest.*

My sister and I looked younger than we were. The three years of hardship under the Nazis had taken their toll in our physical development. Because of this, Mania and Jacob used to be quite unmindful of our presence as they talked, as though we were two little children who did not understand anything. For the first time after what seemed to be many years, Mania and Jacob made us laugh, even though we did not really understand what they were asking of each other and why they were arguing with such heat. Looking back now, it seems to me their behaviour was typical of young people in those days.

One day my sister and I were alarmed when we heard Mania suddenly shout, "Don't touch me! Don't touch me!" Looking in at their door, we saw her dashing around the table, with Jacob in pursuit.

"I'm not going to harm you," he was almost shouting, "but just listen to me." But she would not listen; she seemed beside herself. Finally, when she had lost her breath and stopped running, he was able to say, "But Mania, dear, since we've been left all alone I've tried not to talk about it. But I was sure the problem would arise sooner or later if we stayed together alone under one roof. It's true that the shock of losing one's family will temporarily kill other natural feelings and desires, and maybe this isn't the right time to talk about love when we can't make plans for the future, but please understand me. Our living together this way makes me behave according to my feelings

and not logic. Here we are all alone; I need you and you need me. I love you—in fact, I felt this way the first time I saw you. I really do love you, Mania!"

He stretched his hand out to touch her and at once, alarmed again, Mania ran out of his reach, crying, "No, don't come near me!"

The whole scene struck my sister and me as very comical and we began to laugh. They paid no attention. After a few minutes, when at last Jacob managed to calm her down, she sat quietly beside him. But she said, in an accusing tone of voice, "How dare you suggest such a thing to me? You know I come from a good family and I'm going to remain a virgin until I get married. If I die, I'll die chaste. I'm disappointed in you; I trusted you and didn't expect such behavior from you. I'd rather leave this room, although I've no other place to go, than lead an immoral life, because this would hurt not only me but the memory of my parents."

Jacob listened with a serious expression, assuring her soothingly, "But I didn't mean to hurt you in any way, Mania! I understand perfectly how you feel because we were both brought up in the same way. But you misunderstand me. All I really wanted was to find out how you feel toward me!"

"This is not the time for sentiment and rubbish!" she replied.

"Don't you like me at all?" he persisted wistfully.

Mania hesitated for a brief moment. "I think I do, but my way will be the way of a Jewish girl."

"Good," he exclaimed. "Then I know the solution. Let's go

and get married in the proper Jewish way, and I'll do everything possible to be a good husband to you. Maybe we can't plan for the far future, but perhaps we will be able to save ourselves together."

"All right," she smiled. "But on one condition—that until we're actually married you won't bother me!"

So they decided to go to the office of the Jewish community the very next day to be married. But a couple of hours later they were back, utterly depressed. We were puzzled: was this the way people acted when they got married? My sister thought she knew the reason. "It's because they're alone," she whispered, and I thought she must be right. We therefore went in and congratulated them gaily. "Mazel tov!"

"Hold it," said Mania, gloomily. "We don't have it coming to us."

"What do you mean?" I asked. "Didn't you get married?"

"We couldn't find a rabbi to marry us," Jacob explained.

"Then you won't be able to get married?"

"We don't know as yet. We were given the address of a rabbi who is so sick the Germans haven't bothered with him. We'll go to his house and see."

That evening they were restless and tense and hardly said a word to each other. Next day they again put on their Sabbath clothes and went to see the sick rabbi. They found him lying in bed. "What do you want, children?" he asked weakly when they had knocked and entered his room.

"We are all alone and want to get married," they told him.

He grasped the situation at a glance. "We may well be proud of the daughters of Israel," he whispered. "Some day our entire people will be proud of its children."

"Oh, Rabbi, shall we live to see that moment?" they breathed.

"Hope and faith, my children, are the secret of our existence," he declared. "But now help me up so that I may marry you according to the Law, and may the Almighty bless you."

Chapter Nineteen

Days had passed since our mother's death, and because human beings are so made that they accommodate themselves to almost anything, good or bad, we too adjusted to our reality. Every day when Mania came home from work my sister and I went in to see her. We were very lonely and needed her company. Father was working in Katowitz, a short train-ride from Sosnowiec. From early morning until evening he did hard physical labour in the German food stores without any pay. The only thing he was given in return was fish heads. Instead of throwing them away, he and others were allowed to take them home. We sold them, receiving in exchange some bread, potatoes, sugar and barley. It was our father's standing wish that a few minutes before he was due home we should go outside so that he could see us from a distance. We saw so little of each other that every minute was precious. Each morning when he left our rooms he wondered whether we would still be there when he came back. Leaving us alone this way caused him great anxiety.

Now that our life had become routine, we began to think about other surviving members of our family, particularly the two young cousins who had been hospitalized with typhus. We knew that on the night our mother died, when the nurse's warning had removed us from the hospital in time, a company of SS men had surrounded the building, forbidding anyone to leave. The personnel on duty and all the patients were loaded on trucks and taken directly to the railway station, and from there to Auschwitz. We decided that the next time my aunt Bronka, my mother's youngest sister, came for her weekly visit we must find out what had happened to the boys, for we were very fond of them.

She had quite a story for us. One of the nurses, the one who had warned us in time, was a friend of my aunt's. But it was not possible to remove our two cousins by direct means. After some deliberation between the nurse, the mother and another aunt, it was decided that the only way of saving the boys was to throw them from the third floor and catch them outside. If they could be caught, they would be safe; if not, they were doomed in any event.

During the night the women stood watch near the hospital. The plan was fixed for the early hours of the morning. My aunt was sitting on her children's bed, explaining to them in great detail both the rescue plan and the risks involved. They were only six and eight years old, but she spoke to them as though they were adults, and like adults they listened, promising to be calm and unafraid and exhibiting no sign of panic at the thought of being tossed from a third-storey window.

The hospital was enclosed by a wire fence. According to the plan, their mother was to drop each child and the nurse was to catch them below, tossing each in turn over the fence to where my other aunt would be waiting for them. At dawn, my aunt took her younger son, still wearing his hospital pajamas, and dropped him out the window. The nurse managed to catch him in her arms, giving with the weight so neither of them crashed to the ground, and threw him over the fence. A moment later she had caught the older boy too. They ran quickly to a nearby apartment house, since it was not yet time for the curfew to lift. They reached the house and hurried inside. But once they were all gathered in the hall, my aunt—the long hours of tension over—suddenly went berserk, screaming, "Where are my children? They are gone—where are they?" The two boys hugged her, repeating, "Mother, Mother, here we are, both of us, don't you see us?" But in her frenzy she could neither see nor hear them and was out of her mind with grief. "They've been taken to Auschwitz!" she kept sobbing.

Fortunately there was a doctor in the building. Wakened by the shouting and screaming, the doctor, a Pole, ventured into the hall to investigate. After sizing up the situation he ushered them all into his apartment, where he gave my poor aunt a tranquilizer to quiet her and persuaded her to lie down. Then, giving the two boys food and drink, he provided them with clothes, helped them change and encouraged them with warm, human kindness, and did not spare the Nazi regime his curses. When my aunt was herself again, she thanked the good doctor for his generous help. "Don't you worry," he told her, "because this crime will never be forgotten and they will be punished."

We were much relieved when my aunt Bronka had finished her story. She suggested we visit our grandparents—grandfather had been ill and because of this, they had not reported to the sports stadium. She warned us not to speak of our mother's death. "We have told them she is in the hospital because she broke her leg," she instructed us. "Try to convince them. I'll see you a week from now."

When a week had passed and she did not return, we began to worry. We decided we should call on our grandparents, as she had asked us to do. Besides, they might know what had happened to her. Before entering our grandparents' home we reminded each other of the act we would have to put on.

Trying to assume an expression of cheerfulness, we opened the door and went in. Grandma welcomed us with open arms. "I'm so happy to see you!" she exclaimed, hugging us close. "I've been so worried. How is your mother? How awful that she broke her leg. When did you see her last?"

I could not utter a word but my sister somehow found the strength to speak. "Don't worry, Grandma," she said quite convincingly. "Mother's fine; she'll be well again soon. The doctors are very hopeful. We saw her day before yesterday."

"Now I feel more at ease," said Grandma. "When will you visit her again? I want to go with you."

My heart skipped a beat, but my sister kept her composure. "All right, Grandma, we'll let you know," she said. But grandma began to cry. "Why are you crying? Are you worried about grandpa? How is he now?"

"I can't help weeping—I feel something's wrong," whispered Grandma. "But I do believe you."

"Where is our aunt? Why didn't she come to see us as she promised?" we asked.

"She was caught in the street, taken to the Dolek and sent to Germany." We wrote down her address and went home. Two days later, because grandpa's condition was very bad, we visited grandma again and were faced with the same questions. "Why didn't you take me to see your mother," she complained, her eyes full of foreboding.

"Mother asked us to tell you not to come because you might be caught and sent away. She does not want you to risk your

life for this visit. Soon she'll be well and she will come to see you." I marvelled at my sister's skill. Her love and concern for grandma guided her. Grandma sighed, "*If that is her wish then I shall comply. Besides, I can't leave grandpa in his present state.*"

It was very difficult to go on playing this game, but we had been instructed over and over again by all our relatives to do precisely that. When we were about to leave, grandma urged us to give mother her love, and "Do come and see us again very soon," she said.

Every time we came we brought regards from mother. I had taken hold of myself and, for my family's sake, to prevent their becoming suspicious if I said nothing, contributed my part to this pretense. "Mother asks after you all the time," I assured her, "and about grandpa." Then we would have to invent answers to all the clinical questions she put to us about the care mother was getting and the progress she was making.

Not much later, grandfather died and we accompanied grandma to the cemetery and then back to her home. During the week of mourning people came in at all hours to comfort her. I sat in a corner unobserved and listened to their conversations. Once grandma said, "What sinners we are that we have been made to live in such a time! Hitler has so changed everyone that I don't recognize my own children."

"What do you mean, Leah?" the neighbour asked, and my unhappy grandmother explained, "Well, imagine Ephraim dying and his daughter Esther, who only broke a leg after all, didn't even come to her own father's funeral. She could have come in a wheel-chair! You know, Frieda, how attached we've always been to each other, my Esther and I, so you can

understand how much it hurts . . . ."

Knowing the truth, Frieda tried to calm her. "These are not normal times, Leah; one mustn't judge. If Esther didn't come it was because she couldn't. Of that you may be sure."

I couldn't bear it, so I told my sister it was late and we had better hurry home. "If grandma only knew, she would never forgive herself for saying such things about mother," I told my sister as we walked toward home. Mania saw us and noticed at once that something had disturbed us. We told her the truth. "Don't brood," she urged.

But the next evening she had a more concrete suggestion. "Girls," she called out when she returned from work, "get dressed and I'll take you to a Saturday night show arranged by a very gifted young man, Sroulik Hershkowitz, who makes life easier for Jewish children as long as they are still alive."

It was a most interesting evening. The entertainment included singing in Hebrew and in Yiddish, storytelling and sketches. The hall was filled with children of all ages. Many of us were orphans who had recently lost one or both parents and now had only the parents' clothes to hold close and weep into. We met children there who were only ten years old and taking care of brothers and sisters younger than themselves, being mother and father to them.

Despite these tragic facts, the evening on the whole buoyed us up, arousing in us again the will to live. It was lonely and depressing to come back to an empty home, but we overcame this by going to sleep, willing ourselves to dream of the happier days we had known in the now so distant past.

Chapter Twenty

In October, 1942, the sight of a whole family still alive and together was very rare indeed. One could see a husband without a wife, or a wife without a husband; children orphaned of their parents, parents bereft of their children. Those who were not sent to Auschwitz to be exterminated were transferred to labour camps in Germany. Had there been any possibility of organizing ourselves and obtaining weapons, then everyone, young and old, would have taken vengeance, would have killed, for the blood of the victims and the humiliation served on the Jewish people.

There were, in fact, some young leaders who started to organize. We had a visit from Mordecai Anilewitz, the leader of the Warsaw uprising, who described to us the details of Treblinka and the other death camps. He also described the state of Jews in other parts of Poland, and unanimously we agreed that we had to organize our resistance and plan our rebellion. "The Nazis will kill us all—then let us die honourably," everyone felt.

Anilewitz discussed this also with Moshe Merin and the Judenrat, in the hope of obtaining their consent and assistance; but in this hope he proved wrong. Merin's ideas about a solution to our problems were quite different. He was a pragmatist who looked at the whole matter with practical eyes. "The Nazis' strength and power are unbeatable," he argued. "They are approaching the gates of Stalingrad. Their advance is triumphant.

They have already conquered most of Europe. Great powers cannot resist them. How then can a small number of Jews, unarmed and untrained, without support from anyone outside, surrounded on all sides by enemies, with the world indifferent to their fate or at least keeping silent—how then can we fight them? In a few hours they would finish us off. Rebellion and suicide—and in this case that is just what it would be, suicide—is not always justified. We have to save what we can, even if it should be only a small proportion of our people. Will it be a victory if we all die for the sake of our honour? No, the only purpose it will serve is Hitler's. It will help him achieve his aim. No, it won't do, especially since Dreier has promised me that those who remain here will be saved." Merin really believed in the enemy's false promises, he was really convinced that his brand of realism was the only way to look at things.

But this did not placate Anilewitz and his colleagues. Under the leadership of Zvi Dunsky, Lippa Mintz, Heller Schnitzer, and Joseph Kosak, the Sosnowiec group aimed at a genuine resistance, maintaining communications with Warsaw. They printed circulars which they clipped into boots being shipped to the front; printed, and posted on walls, manifestos against the regime and the Judenrat. They even plotted to kill Moshe Merin.

Merin was busy too. He set up a network of spies, who infiltrated the organization and reported back to him. As soon as he had enough names, he made his move. He rounded up all the resistance people and had them transferred to camps in Germany.

Thus our first attempt to organize an uprising locally was shattered at its inception. Now the Jews were too numb to care. Some of the young continued their determined attempt to organize, insisting that the Germans were only "mortals like ourselves. The same bullets can smash their heads too." But, they had no bullets. So they were shipped off to German camps without getting their chance to fight back.

Once again people were ordered to report to have their certificates stamped. This time the Nazis realized that none of us would come of our own accord. They therefore decided on the next step—to concentrate all the Jews in one area. The ghetto for Sosnowiec was instituted.

The order was issued. A few miles from Sosnowiec there was a suburb named Shrodule. All the non-Jewish residents were ordered out, and in exchange they were given the Jewish homes in the city. We packed our things and prepared to be transferred. My sister and I were among the first to go. In packing I came upon a big surprise, a WILL AND TESTAMENT handwritten on page after page by my mother. There was no time to read it now, so I packed it with the rest of my things to read after reaching the ghetto.

We spent the first day there resting, for it had been quite a job for two young girls to carry everything to the ghetto. Worn out, we went to sleep early, thinking and dreaming only of—freedom, vengeance, a better future . . . Then, after catching my breath in our new room, I took out the tightly written pages and began to read. Once I had started I could not stop. I cannot recall everything in detail, but let me set down the main points in my mother's will which reflected our life in the past and spoke for all those who were no more.

Chapter Twenty-One

She began by stating that she was writing on behalf of the dead and dying Jews. Recent events—the Nazis' victories and their atrocities—had created an increasing sense of insecurity. She had, she explained, a clear premonition that all the Jews of Poland would be destroyed, and she hoped that one day Jews all over the world would read these pages, learn from the mistakes of the past, and respect the will of all those who had paid with their lives for being Jews.

"Hatred of the Jews, with all its ugly facets, existed before Hitler. His crimes were not spontaneous acts but the result of generations of incitement, which aided Hitler in executing his crimes against the Jewish people. There are many reasons for this hatred: ignorance; the dispersion of the Jews for two thousand years among many nations, without having a homeland of their own, becoming easy scapegoats to divert public opinion from other problems; prejudice; and malicious slander. The Jews became collectively responsible for the crimes of individuals, and were beaten for their weaknesses as well as for their stubborness. We suffered because of our inclination towards separatism; but attempts to assimilate did not help either. We were persecuted when we helped to build the economy *of a country and for excelling in scientific and cultural fields. Every state failure was attributed to us and we had to suffer silently until the storm was over. It was always the same problem—now in one country, now in another."*

"But now, in the twentieth century, when everybody speaks so highly of human rights, progress, freedom of speech, and social equality, how indifferent is the world when we are taken by trains to our death, lonely and frustrated. The extermination of the Jews, it seems, is considered to be a side effect of the war and not to be brought into the strategical calculations; and nobody raises a finger to help us. Every power, big or small, strong or weak, that can limit the scope of the holocaust and does not, is an accomplice. Up to now we have not seen even one power come to our rescue. Nobody is stretching a helping hand, nobody tries to assist us. They watch us being led to death as if we were vermin. Only very few still behave like human beings, but even these do not dare to give vent to what they think or feel."

"In one word: the only solution to our problem is self-emancipation."

"Faith keeps us alive, but we do not understand why we are punished so, why we are being destroyed. What crimes have we committed that such monsters can rise up to annihilate us? Only because the Jews do not have a land and a state of their own can this happen."

"God gave the right to live in freedom and happiness to everybody. Everybody was born equal."

"Individually we Jews were very clever, but collectively we were stupid. We thought that everything would be all right, without changing the basic reason for our plight. We must live without illusions and without delusions. Our past is tragic, but we should not fail in the future."

"Our only consolation is that maybe in other countries Jews are still free to live their real Jewish life, and when we are gone they will remember us. Only God knows that we had no alternative, and those who save themselves will perhaps be able to explain why we did not uprise and rebel. They will tell you that we tried, though we knew we had no chance. If the Jewish youth will know the truth about this horrible epoch they will understand that we did not bring shame and humiliation on the Jewish people the way we died. They will know that the Jews of Europe went to their deaths without resistance because they were broken, and not because they did not have the courage to fight for their lives. We are united in our deaths. Be you united in life. This is the will of the dead."

This was the will of the little child who did not know how to explain himself, but whose eyes expressed all that he was feeling. This was the will of the older children whose eyes spoke expressly of what they wanted. I heard the same words from the doomed who were transferred to Targowa Street under *heavy guard before being sent to Auschwitz. I heard this last will and testament in the ghetto, in labour camps and death camps, from those who died from starvation, hard labour, and disease. I was part of them, and I want to communicate what they and I felt we must express to the fortunate ones who escaped the holocaust.*

Chapter Twenty-Two

When I finished reading my mother's will I was dizzy with emotion and confusion: the future was unknown and the reality of the ghetto, its hunger, the density, the sickness, was unbearable.

It was afternoon. Impatiently I waited for father to come home from his work. He always brought some food and a little money from the sale of the fish heads. With this money we were able to buy rations. My mood invariably improved after I had something to eat—maybe my feeling of hopelessness would lift.

After reading my mother's will I suffered from insomnia, but otherwise our existence continued in the same pattern. Life in the ghetto was designed to break us, and it swept away any illusions we had left. Every day provided new corpses for the graves. We were sick, we starved, and we lived in terror of death day and night. The children looked bizarre, as though arrived from the valley of death, emaciated and covered in rags. The same news occupied the centre of attention every day: who had been sent away, who had died, who still remained, who would be the next victim. It is hard to describe the feeling of waiting, realizing that the next day or next week one might in all likelihood be dead, knowing the form that death would take. This was excruciating mental agony, in some ways worse than death itself. But this was our reality. We had no hope of help. This illusion was now gone. The only help we could still hope for was the divine help of God. This hope we still nurtured.

Every night before falling asleep, I silently said a simple prayer that I might be saved from the Nazis' claws. Whenever I sensed an especially bad mood overtaking the ghetto, I would beg only that if I had to die, death would come quickly, unexpectedly—only not by the gas of Auschwitz!

During the day we were alone, waiting for father to come back so that we might talk a little. Perhaps he might even bring a bit of encouraging news. "What's the news today, Father?" we would ask him. One day he smiled bitterly at this question and said, "What irony! I saw a headline in a German paper, a huge banner headline that read 'THE GREATEST CRIME OF THE ALLIES: CIVILIANS KILLED BY BOMBS ON GERMANY!'" We burst out laughing—the poor Germans, how terribly they were being treated . . . .

Father was still working at the German food depot. He had managed to get a blue certificate with the letter "A" on it, which should have been our best security against expulsion.

One early morning in October father went to work as usual. My sister and I were still asleep when he left and he did not want to wake us. He left without making any noise. When we woke up, we dressed and went out to roam a bit in the ghetto streets.

Near one of the houses we saw a group of little children playing. The game was called "Expulsion". One of them imitated the gait and speech of Dreier, while some of the others pretended to be SS men, and the rest, bending beneath imaginary bundles on their backs, were supposed to be Jews. They were enacting the expulsion scenes we all knew too well. The children with bundles were running while the "Nazis" pursued them, beating them with sticks, shooting them with pointed fingers, shouting, "Quick! Quick! " in German. This was a common game in the ghetto streets. The tragedy of their innocent play-acting impressed on our consciousness a reality we tried to put from our minds. We looked at them for a moment with a sense of overwhelming grief and then hurried away. We soon turned back toward home. Looking at the clock, we saw it was only two; father would return at six—four hours to wait. We waited and waited that day, but he failed to come at six or at seven. We stood outside the door until very late, but—no father. What had happened?

We tried to eat something and lay down in our bed. Early in the morning we hurried to the offices of the Judenrat to find out what had happened. The offices were still locked. We went to the homes of others who had husbands or sons working with father, but none of them knew anything. We reappeared at the Judenrat. "The group that worked in Katowitz? " the clerk repeated. "Oh, yes, beginning on the first of November Jews will not be allowed to go to work by train out of town. Therefore, all of those working in Katowitz were taken to the Dolek and sent to a labour camp in Germany. No, they were not given the chance to take personal belongings or to say goodbye to anyone."

"To what camp? " we asked anxiously.

Looking at his notes, the clerk replied, "We don't know. But what is encouraging is that the German labour camps are at least safe. Remember that." And because he was aware of our distress, the clerk repeated this fact several times.

We left the office in silence. Looking at each other, we saw the *same question in our eyes: what were we going to do now? Taking myself in hand, I tried to console my sister. "At least he was sent to a labour camp. In our position that is the best place for him." But what are we going to do now, I kept asking myself, though I did not say it aloud.*

After two or three days we were completely out of food. There was not a crumb of anything. The little money we had was gone. We began to sell the bits of clothing and other belongings we had left in order to buy our weekly rations, but very soon this too was finished. The day I so dreaded came: we had absolutely nothing to eat. We went about all day with nothing to put in our mouths. In the evening my sister said, "I'm hungry. I won't be able to sleep, I'm so hungry."

"I have nothing to give you," I replied, feeling responsible for her because she was the younger. "Tomorrow we'll go to our friends. Maybe we'll get something to eat."

We went to bed. I knew why she could not fall asleep. I myself fell asleep only toward morning. Lying awake in the dark, I made some important decisions about the next day and I thought hard about the future. We are like animals in a jungle, I thought, for here too the weak are the first to be annihilated. But hunger, I discovered, was stronger than the fear of death. I made up my mind to go to the Judenrat kitchen to ask for soup, a step I had heretofore refrained from taking, because I no longer had any faith in people. I had been disillusioned at too young an age; I tended now to suspect everyone's motives. I realized that joining the soup-line would place us among the weak—the Judenrat had to provide the Germans with a list of those receiving the soup, and I did not want our names on any list. But when hunger gnaws at your vitals you can think of nothing else. When life becomes too terrible a burden, I philosophised, perhaps it is, after all, for the best; it will not be so hard to give it up—let the end come. Thinking these thoughts I finally fell asleep and did not wake in the morning until there was a knock at the door and a middle-aged man walked in. He looked about fifty years old, and he carried a note in his hand.

"My name is Gritzer," he introduced himself. "I was sent here by the Judenrat. Your father was sent to a labour camp and I am supposed to live here with you in his place."

"You are welcome," we replied. In the ghetto one room never served only two people. We would be lucky if they did not send us more. "There will be plenty of room for all three of us," we assured him. He told us he was left all alone; his entire family was dead. Asking us for our names, he arranged his belongings. He was a nice man, serious and polite. More than that we did not know about him.

We got up and dressed but somehow felt we could not go to the Judenrat kitchen. Perhaps we should try to find some food elsewhere. We started on a round of visits to acquaintances, and whenever they asked how we were, we hinted at the purpose of our visit. They gave us what they could; nobody had food to spare. Some days we had nothing to eat at all and went about all day hungry, apathetic, pale and hopeless. When my head was very dizzy I knew that, sooner or later, we would have to go to the Judenrat kitchen to ask for their miserable soup, no matter what the result. I therefore had a strong urge for someone close to us, as if to say goodbye. I thought of my aunt Bronka, who had been sent to a labour camp in Germany, and found her address. I decided to explain to her our position and suggest that she try to persuade her camp manager to accept us into Camp Waldenburg as workers, despite our youthful ages, for the place was reputed to be quite humane. The next evening, my paper and envelope in hand, I asked Mr. Gritzer to lend me his pen. "What are you going to write?" he asked.

"A letter to my mother's sister," I replied. "She is at Waldenburg and I want her to arrange to have us taken in as labourers. It is my only hope for leaving the ghetto. The earth is burning under our feet."

I had no sooner said this than he jumped to his feet and began to pace up and down the room in a frenzy, repeating over and over, "No, no, they have no right! The Nazis have no right to kill you . . . But who is going to stop them? You are so young. I don't think you have any chance of being admitted to a labour camp . . . Why? Why?" He was beside himself.

I thought he had lost his mind, and I was quite frightened. Then suddenly there was a knock at the door. In came a friend of Mr. Gritzer's. Looking first at him and then at us, he sat down with a sigh. "What's happened to you, Haim?"

"They have no right, do you hear!" And then he added, "They don't stand a chance, David. What do you think?" And with a visible effort to calm down he sat beside his friend and explained my plan to him. They discussed it between them earnestly. "We have failed in everything," Mr. Gritzer said to his friend.

"Let me bring my niece, Helenka," offered David. "She smuggles weapons from Warsaw to us. She is our communications link with them."

Mr. Gritzer exploded again, "The time for talk is over. There is nothing to do but fight. History will not forgive us if we merely suffer in silence. As long as we are sane, we have to do what our self-respect demands of us."

David answered him, "Come, my friend, wake up to reality. If you mean that we ought to rebel, then I can tell you something. I know a little about the organization my niece is helping to arm. They have five revolvers! Can you stage a rebellion with five pistols? Against all the machine guns, tanks, bombs; without any help from outside, to fight with bare hands? They will finish us off in a few hours. If they had come to take all of us at one go, I would have been the first to organize such an uprising, for it would represent a final desperate chance. But as it is, there is always a slim chance—as long as a person is alive he hopes for the impossible to happen...."

Mr. Gritzer cut him off. "You're quite right. They will not come to take us all at once. Again they will take a group of women, children," and here he stole a sad glance at us, "and some old people. The women will resist, trying to protect the children, while the old, fed up with life, will wish to die as soon as possible. The rest they will beat up or kill outright, and the last remnants will be shipped off to Auschwitz and arrive there half dead. Can we let this crime continue? Can we?"

"Calm down, Haim, calm down. We shall hear many encouraging details from my niece, Helenka. I'll bring her to meet you as soon as she returns from a meeting of the heads of the organization; she is reporting what is going on all over the Polish ghettos, about the preparations in Warsaw, about the contacts with the outside world—everything."

Then he rose and left. I could not concentrate on writing my letter; my head was spinning with all I had heard. The details he had promised concerned us personally, too, for I hoped they might give me some indication of a way out for us, or a measure of consolation or encouragement. Perhaps hope was still possible....

Our ghetto was still what was known as "open"—people could enter and leave it without running into too much trouble. So it was late that evening when the guests arrived. David came back, accompanied by his wife and his niece, Helenka, a pretty girl of eighteen, very alert, with big green eyes and long blonde hair. She did not look Jewish and was able to move around the country without arousing immediate suspicion. She greeted us in a friendly way, and her uncle made the introductions. "This is my very good friend, Haim, and these are two orphans who are very bright. You can speak freely here, you are among friends."

"What would you like to know?" she responded. "I shall answer any question I can."

Mr. Gritzer jumped right in. "Do we have a chance? If not, we should do everything to save our honour at least. We are lost in any case. At least let future generations know we fought to the end. If we cannot live, let us die in dignity. That's what I feel. Helenka, you and I know that many others feel the same way, but your uncle does not agree."

Before she could comment, her uncle spoke up. "You did not understand me," he said. "I am not against self-defence, only against suicide which gives no chance of killing even one Nazi. But let's hear what Helenka has to say."

She seemed to take little notice of the argumentative stance of Mr. Gritzer and her uncle, but quickly spoke out. "First of all," she said, "I can tell you where we are most active right now—in the sector previously occupied by the Russians, which is now in

German hands; Central Poland, which the Germans call the General Government; and in your area, Upper Silesia."

She glanced at my sister and me and then went into details of the early events after the invasion; facts which we had already heard from distraught survivors, but which now took on a new clarity as she recounted them quickly and calmly.

"In the parts they took from Russia they shot Jews down with machine guns beside ditches that served as mass graves. This was really the first of the mass executions, although no one knew it then. Whole towns were wiped out. People went to their deaths without knowing what was happening to them. The Nazis managed to mislead and deceive them until the last minute. Their method was to surround a district with Ukrainians and other collaborators who caused such terror that people preferred dying rather than enduring their brutality."

"And when people discovered the truth, what then?" asked Mr. Gritzer.

"We organized ourselves," was her decisive reply. "In Wilno, for instance, the United Partisans Organization still carries on an underground battle against the Nazis. In Cracow the first fighting unit was set up in 1941. Other towns and cities have organized their own units too. One group is not aware of the other's existence, they only know they must do something to defend themselves. There has been no central guidance—and that is what my job is: to make sure each group knows the others exist, and where, and what they are doing. The partisan fighters of East Poland were lucky. They managed to forge a link with the Red Army and they hold on, carrying out acts of sabotage that the Germans are really feeling. Some of them are bound to survive until the liberation." Helenka paused for a moment and

I could feel a tingle of hope growing in me. People in our ghetto had such a hopeless outlook that just hearing someone speak the words "bound to survive" revived my imagination.

Then Helenka continued. "Not all of our people have been so lucky. Many Jews tried escaping to the forests with the help of Polish guides. But too often they were abandoned without making contact with the underground. On the contrary, at times the guide betrayed them to the Germans and they would all be killed. The lot of the Jewish partisans who escaped the ghettos of Central Poland is very bitter. They come in contact with the Polish Popular Fighting Forces, who often as not betray them and have even murdered them on occasion, impelled by a blind hatred of Jews."

"But we have had our successes too. The unit in Cracow attacked storehouses of weapons, set fire to military warehouses, hurled hand grenades into the German cafe Tzigane, killing twenty Nazis and wounding many more. The Nazis' own game of propaganda is beginning to backfire. We do it too. In the town of Brody we have a phenomenal group of fighters. Some of them succeeded in getting to the forests, others stayed back in the ghetto and continue to fight there. Together with the group from L'vov they blew up a factory near Sokolovka and attacked a quarry in Svosov for the purpose of taking their explosives. They got fifty kilos of dynamite and blew up a train with it, killing many Germans. But we don't have the minimal conditions that can lead to large-scale victories. God knows our people have shown real courage. On the Purim holiday the Nazis selected ten Jews to be hanged but they continued to dance and· sing right up until the very last moment. One of them, Shlomo, sang with all his might and confounded the Germans. That was in Merdinska Volia. A group of Hassidic Jews were caught in a cellar in Cracow and they broke into Hassidic dances to show

their murderers the Jewish spirit could not be broken."

Again Helenka paused, and seemed to reflect for a moment. "We know very well," she continued with a nod, "what is going on in Central Poland. We know there are many extermination camps there—Treblinka for Warsaw and Bialystok districts, Sobivor for Lublin and Keltz, Belsec for the province of Galicia, Majdanek and Auschwitz for Upper Silesia and the Third Reich. To Treblinka and Auschwitz come trains from all parts of Europe. They deal with the European Jews differently than with us. Oh yes—we know—they are all told a carefully calculated lie, that they are being transferred to the East for resettlement. They are told to take all their belongings except for furniture. So the poor souls pack fine suitcases, dress themselves well, and board passenger trains which seem quite free except for the military escort accompanying them. The trains stop now and then, and they receive food and drink to prevent their becoming suspicious. Some ask the soldiers the name of the new settlement and are told 'Treblinka'. 'Is it much further?' they ask, not knowing that it will be the furthest point in their lives."

"When they reach Treblinka, one car is detached from the rest of the train and its passengers are told to put all their luggage in a certain place, undress and, 'after such an exhausting trip', take a shower. They are led then into elevators which bring them into the gas chambers and crematoria. When our people warned them, they refused to believe them. They thought us mad. Often people approach them, residents of Malkin and Kossov, two villages between which Treblinka was built. 'Give us whatever you have,' they demand, 'you'll be killed here anyway.' The poor people think they want to rob them of their possessions; so they don't even listen and are brought to their death without the slightest resistance.

"We Polish Jews, however, are treated quite differently. With us they don't pretend anymore. You have all seen, with your own eyes, their brutality. Their aim is to break our spirit and morale so that they will be able to carry out their program of extermination without any resistance."

She fell silent. Then David asked, "Helenka, how do the Poles react now that they know what is happening to us? Is their attitude any better now?"

"All I know," she answered, "is that a few want to help us and some even risk their lives to do so. But the majority do not care at all. We feel very much alone. I have contacts with the Polish underground, and we have talked about it. They did contact General Sikorsky in London for us and he informed the world of the atrocities here. But as you know—we are still waiting. Many of these underground fighters say they are ashamed to be human beings when they see what the Germans are doing, ashamed to be Poles when they see how their own people betray us, even ashamed to be Christians when they see the condition of the world after two thousand years of their faith. Yes, they are ashamed . . . but we are being killed."

"So what have you and your comrades decided to do?" asked Mr. Gritzer.

"We are going to fight. We know this is only the beginning of the total extermination of the Jews. It is only a question of time. We do not agree that we should wait in silence. There is nothing that can stop us from reacting in the only way left to us—stand up and fight. We want to help organize resistance in every ghetto, but there are difficulties. The main source for buying and manufacturing arms is in Warsaw. In other ghettos, especially the small ones, there is no such possibility, and the transfer of every single rifle involves tremendous complications and risk. Then, too, we are not prepared or trained in any way for such a mission. Most of our people are teachers, pedagogues, rather than soldiers, and they hesitate to take the responsibility of leading young men and women into actual fire. But we are overcoming this problem too. We train the young people in Warsaw in the use of firearms and then send them out to other ghettos to head the movements for the final struggle. But the main difficulties are still the lack of arms and the opposition from within to our plan. Many believe we have no chance at all and that by not resisting at least some will survive. But we, the young in every ghetto, hope to persuade them that our way is right. We know there is no help from the outside, but a few of us will make it through."

Mr. Gritzer became excited again. "I can't understand it," he shouted. "How can the so-called enlightened world look on at such sub-human deeds and not move a finger! They all know the truth, they have agents everywhere, the Red Cross has its representatives in Germany. They hear us crying for help and they do nothing."

Nobody said a word. It was late. They got up to leave.

"I have to leave the ghetto by the first train in the morning," Helenka told her uncle.

"Don't forget us," he begged.

"I shall not forget," she promised.

"Please take care of yourself. Even though you pass for a Polish girl, I shan't close my eyes tonight for worry about you."

"Don't you worry, I'll manage. I've been in danger before."

The young girl behaved like a woman of much experience. We bade one another goodbye with the hope that we would all meet again to enjoy the defeat of the Nazis.

Chapter Twenty-Three

Two of Helenka's assertions remained fixed in my mind: "Some Poles want to help . . . A few even risk their lives to save us." A wild thought took hold of me—perhaps our Polish neighbours have changed their attitude. Maybe, now that they have seen the magnitude of our situation, they understand we have one common enemy. After all, their own position is not so good either. The Nazis oppress them more and more. And besides, I urged myself, what can we possibly lose in our desperate circumstances? The condemned have nothing to lose.

I did not shut my eyes throughout the night. Getting out of my bed, I studied myself in the mirror. Nothing suspicious in my appearance. Although my eyes were brown, my hair was fair, and I did not look Jewish. But going back to bed, I looked at my sister with her dark hair and brows. I hesitated but was determined not to give up my plan.

Next morning I told my sister what I had in mind; she approved. We put on clothes and hats to cover all we could of ourselves, being sure some of my blonde hair showed. As it was a cold December day, there was nothing in that to arouse suspicion. We stole out of the ghetto; we knew every road and path inside and outside the town, and we made our way quickly to the village that was our destination. We knocked at the door of a Polish woman, a friend from before the war. Seeing us, she crossed herself and exclaimed, "Jesus Christ, Holy Mother, are you still *alive?"*

"Yes," we answered, "we are still alive." But suddenly a cold sweat covered my whole body. She sat us down at the table and gave us some hot soup. As we ate, I hinted at the purpose of our visit. Her lips tight, she let us finish eating and then said abruptly, "You must leave this minute, I don't want you to endanger my family!" We put our coats on and left.

We hurried along, but whenever we saw children playing in the snow we turned and walked in the opposite direction, lest they recognize us and start shouting "Jews!" They did this automatically, so acclimatized were they to Nazi propaganda.

We went to see another Polish woman we knew. When she opened the door she turned deathly pale. "How did you manage to get out of the ghetto?" she whispered.

"We sneaked out," we replied.

"And where do you expect to hide?"

"We don't know," I said. "We're looking for someone who will be ready to hide us."

"You can't expect that. You know that if they find someone hiding Jews, they kill him and his whole family. The Germans have offered rewards to anyone informing on Poles who hide Jews, and you know there will always be some scoundrel to inform for the sake of the reward." She gave us each a piece of bread and hinted we had better go.

We went yet to another family we had known for years. She was a nice lady and asked us many questions, but it was obvious she was very uneasy. The slightest noise, even of her own children in another room, made her tremble with fear. Seeing her fright we realized she would not let us stay, and we were only keeping her and ourselves under a terrible nervous strain. We put on our coats and left.

We decided to try someone we didn't know. We went off to another village and knocked on the door of a sharecropper's house. The wife answered and we asked her whether she did not need help in the house. "Yes," she replied, "But not from Jews. Go back to the ghetto where you belong!"

It was growing dark and we had no place to sleep. I decided we must go once again to Maria. Quickening our pace almost to a run we headed for Maria's house. It was bitter cold and we were freezing. We knocked at the door, but the woman who opened it was a stranger. We inquired about Maria.

"Oh yes, they moved to a new flat."

"Where?"

"I don't know. Tomorrow I'll find out and tell you."

I was desperate, for we did not have a night's lodging. I remembered the hostility of Maria's neighbours and did not dare knock at their doors. With no alternative, we had to stay right there and sleep in the stairway. We sat under the stairs, off in a corner, and huddled in the dark, freezing cold. Tired beyond words, we said nothing lest someone hear us and turn us in for the reward. Bitterly I thought to myself, if those who could have prevented this could see us now, at this very moment, they would understand the magnitude of their shortsightedness—I could never forgive them for it, their hands would never be washed of it. I could not, of course, close my eyes all night and sat there thinking and thinking. Could we possibly save ourselves? "No," I thought, "there is no hope of surviving the many days to come before liberation. If our close friends won't help us, who will? We won't last long if we beg for food in the daytime and sleep in stairwells at night. At any moment a child may point at us and cry out 'Jew!', and then a German patrol will materialize out of thin air. Either one of the police dogs will tear us to pieces, or the man will be kind and put a bullet in our heads. Any day, any minute. Who is a friend? Who is an enemy? We don't even know anymore."

In the meantime, every slightest sound made us hold our breath, trembling with terror. That night seemed years long. With every passing minute my conviction grew that we had no chance. We had not found, and would not find, the "few who were ready to help us." Not in this neighbourhood anyway. We had to go back to the ghetto.

It was a long time since I had felt so happy when we reached our small room in the ghetto, with its bed and warm blanket, and friends sharing our common lot. With great relief we went to bed. Hours later, in the evening, I decided to write the letter to my aunt.

Early in the evening Mr. Gritzer came back from work and was glad to see us safe and sound in the room. He had been worried about us and wanted to know where we had been. We told him and he remarked, "If you had only asked my advice, I could have saved you all the misery of yesterday. Helenka's talk convinced you there were noble-minded people still to be found. I hope she is right, but there are also many without conscience."

Then he told us this story: Not far from the little town of

Olkush the Germans rounded up all the Jews to have them sent away. One mother, desperately wanting to save her child, told her to run away, to go as far as she could and then ask some Polish family to take her in as their daughter. She was a clever little girl of eight, and she managed to steal away. She was wearing a nice summer dress. In a village she knocked on one of the doors. An old woman appeared. "Grandma," the child appealed to her, "will you take me for your daughter?" The old woman did not think; automatically she called a Nazi soldier. Taking away the child's dress, she said to him, "Here's a Jewish girl." The German shot the child on the spot. The old woman did not expect that, she thought he would simply take the child away; and she could find no peace. She went to her priest for confession.

"You did a very bad thing," he told her. "You should have given the child the refuge she was looking for, or at least you should have let her go to look for it elsewhere. You did a very wicked thing. Jesus will not forgive you and I cannot take your guilt on my conscience." The old woman went home and, after a short time, she died.

"We almost met the same fate," I told him, "except that our woman said, 'Go back to the ghetto where you belong!'"

Mr. Gritzer sighed and shook his head, "Will anyone ever believe this. . . ."

"I cannot do anything more, except write my letter," I said. Before the words were out of my mouth, the door flew open and in came David, looking almost happy.

"You look pleased, David. What's the good news?" Mr. Gritzer greeted him.

"I came to share my joy with you. I just got a message that Helenka arrived in Warsaw safely, thank God."

We were all pleased. I remembered Helenka well. She had fascinated me with her energy, her sense of purpose. So I asked David, "Who is Helenka? I mean, how did she become involved in her work? It's so dangerous! "

Mr. Gritzer nodded, "Yes, David, I'm curious. You once said you thought she had gone in the wrong direction, she was a failure, I think you said. Why? I wish we had more like her. I think she is a triumph, not a failure. Anyway, you're obviously very fond of her."

"Alright, I'll tell you," David said. "You're right, Haim. I am very fond of Helenka. It's a long story, but I'll tell you briefly so you'll understand what I mean. When my younger brother, Helenka's father, finished his studies and became a lawyer, he married and moved to Warsaw. Having been persecuted at the university because he was a Jew, he now tried to become assimilated. He and his wife estranged themselves from everything Jewish—religion, environment, tradition, society. They joined those secular circles that believed in building a new world of freedom and justice through abolishment of all national differences, by assimilation into the general mainstream. I don't have to tell you the results of this attempt. They ended up in the ghetto like all the rest of us. When Helenka came to visit us I was, of course, happy to see her, but terribly worried about the risks she was running. 'Why do you endanger your life all the time? ' I asked her. 'Don't your parents object to what you are doing? ' "

" 'Yes, they do,' she answered me, 'especially mother. She keeps trying to persuade me to give it up; she's tried everything, but *it's no use. And I must admit, although it is not the reason I joined the underground, I do feel glad I can get back at my parents in this way. Had my father been an uneducated man, busy all the time trying to earn a living for his family, I'd certainly have forgiven him. But for a man like him, a well-known lawyer, to have been so short-sighted—this I cannot forgive. Today I know that my own parents denied me all the joy in life. When the Nazis ordered us to move into the ghetto, they didn't ask who is a religious Jew, who is a progressive, who is assimilated. We were all equal, all simply Jews. They reminded everybody of the irrefutable fact that you can't deny your identity or avoid your destiny. In the ghetto I've come to know young Jews who are educated and believe in ideals. There is nothing more beautiful,'* she said, *'than to believe in some sacred ideal, in the welfare of your own people. That's how I feel. My parents were cowards, afraid they might be recognized as Jews. I'm glad to be one. You can't imagine how happy I am to observe the Jewish holidays! It makes me feel I belong! Only now do I feel really alive, normal, healthy—only since our arrival in the ghetto. Yes, my parents did not let me live as a proud Jew; let me at least die as one, I tell them. But I agreed to do one favour for my mother: I carry a poison pill with me. If ever they catch me, I'll rob them of the pleasure of torturing me to death.'*"

"So you see, Haim, isn't it a failure to have grown up with so little respect for your parents?"

"It is our failure that we did not give them reason to respect us—we did not teach them to fight back. We urged them always to submit quietly. We must not be passive or indulge in self-pity anymore," Mr. Gritzer replied.

Thus another evening passed, and I did not write my letter but sat instead listening attentively to the talk of the grownups. But in the morning, I resolved to write my aunt, else it might be too late. I was desperate and I did not hide it from her:

> Dear Aunt,
> I feel I must speak to someone who is close to me, and it may even be the letter of our parting. I see no possibility of our being saved. The situation in the ghetto is growing worse day by day. We live in constant terror, insecurity and hunger. We no longer have any faith in German certificates. Father has been taken to a German labour camp and we are alone, without any resources, and starving. People are turning into beasts. Any day now the Nazis may come and round us up for Auschwitz. We live here as in a jungle, the weak are taken first. The only hope we cling to is that maybe you could ask the people responsible for your camp to take us in as additional workers. If we have food to eat we will work hard. Although we are young we will try to do any kind of work. But in case they will deny your application, I want to part from you and wish you health.
> Take care of yourself,
Chava

I sealed the envelope, wrote the address and headed for the Judenrat, to the department for the dispatch of letters and parcels, and delivered my letter. For some reason, perhaps because the Germans were so certain their plan to liquidate the Jews would be successful, there was no longer much problem in mail delivery to and from the camps. Then, walking quickly, I turned toward home. But suddenly I was stopped in the street. Caught up in someone's arms, I was being hugged and kissed. When they released me for a second, I saw my two girl-friends, Zosia and Tosia. "Oh! " I exclaimed. "I'm so happy to see you! When did you arrive? "

"A few days ago."

I invited them to come with me to our room so we could chat undisturbed. Once there I told them about the letter I had just posted.

"I don't want to destroy your hopes, dear," Tosia said quietly, "but these are delusions, just wishful thinking. You know they admit only people who are at least eighteen years old. You and your sister are much too young and you look even younger than you are."

This depressed me greatly, but then I said, "It was the only thing left to try, our only chance! At least I shall know I tried everything I could . . . . And who is left of your family, Zosia? "

"Only my brother and I," she replied, her eyes full of tears. "My mother and father did everything they could to save us but they lost their own lives. Ever since then I can't stop crying."

"But how do you manage with your brother? He is only six years old, isn't he? "

"You wouldn't believe it. That little boy has turned overnight into an adult. Even though he misses mother and father terribly. Every little while he comes over to me, kisses me without a word. I'm only twelve myself and need my parents too, but what can I do? I try to be mother and father to him. Of one thing you may be sure: whatever happens to him will happen to me too."

"Zosia," I asked my friend, "if you survive until the liberation comes, what do you think you will do then?"

She reflected for a moment and then said, "I was only nine years old when the war broke out and I hadn't had much time in school. When these terrible things started to happen, I kept asking myself over and over again — are we really different? Are we really inferior? And if we are not, why are we being killed simply because we are Jews? I began to read a lot, every book I could get my hands on, and it gave me some of the answers. Little by little I freed myself of the sense of being inferior. I think I'd devote my life to finding out what are the reasons for our persecution and what is the solution."

"I would, too," I agreed. "I would not even get married."

"I would," Tosia broke in, "because I'm not smart enough to function in that direction on my own. I'd find a clever husband to help me...."

We laughed, and we all thought how much better it was to laugh than to cry.

I had not asked my other friend how things were with her, so I said to Tosia, "And what about you—who has remained in your family?"

"My little sister—she's four years old—and my brother, who is eight," she answered.

"And your parents?"

"Gone. They too did everything to save us. All the mothers were like that."

"And how do you manage, Tosia?"

"I've become a smuggler and I make a living for us."

"But you may be killed any day, any time!"

"Of course. I know that. But do I have an alternative? I prefer to die than to see my brother and sister starve. Every time they hug and kiss me and say 'we love you', I get new courage to go on with my job. True, many a night I lie awake, thinking that this terrible world is not worth living in . . . ."

Having unburdened ourselves a little, I suggested we go to the Judenrat, where every day new people were arriving. Out we went and when we walked into the centre we were still deep in conversation. We did not notice, but one of the adults had been listening to us as we talked. He approached us, a sad and defeated man, and without any preliminaries said, "Children, forgive us. We intellectuals were wrong. We didn't want to recognize our responsibility. We were looking only for our own solutions without taking into account our responsibility to the future generations—to you children. Now I look at you—there is not much more I can say. If we had another chance we would be the most demanding of Zionists. But there will be no more chances. Forgive us. It will be easier for us to die if we know you forgive us." As children, we did not understand all his words, but I am not sure we forgave him, or the people he was pleading for.

He disappeared into the crowd and the noise and we looked around. I realized at once from the people's expressions that some special news had been received. I approached and listened. A group of our people, I found out, had been taken from Auschwitz to work outside the camp. On the second day, encountering some Polish passers-by on their way, they managed to write on little bits of paper what was happening in Auschwitz and threw them down near the Poles. They, in turn, sold the bits of paper to Jews. They told of horrors that were already known to most people, but for me they were new and they terrified me beyond words. When they reached Auschwitz, the prisoners reported on these papers, they were met by the infamous Dr. Mengele and his staff, who proceeded to select victims for their medical experiments. He liked to seize from the lines of Jews all twins and all children who did not look typically Jewish, especially those with blue eyes and black hair, or with brown eyes and blond hair. They were taken to special barracks where experiments were performed on them without the aid of anesthetics. The screams of the tortured children were so agonizing that many of our people who were quartered nearby threw themselves at the electrified barbed wire, or went out of their minds. When the doctors were finished with them, they threw the children, half-conscious and still alive, into the crematorium.

Hearing this I began to tremble. My appearance made me a certain candidate for such tortures. Now it was no longer a matter of dying, but how I would die. I prayed constantly that I might be lucky enough to die an easier, quicker death. At night I would dream I was standing in line and Dr. Mengele was pointing at me, ordering me out of line. I would begin to scream in my sleep and wake up in a cold sweat.

Unnerving as my visits to the Judenrat were, I kept going back. It was always crowded and noisy. New people arrived every hour and it was the centre for news, new rumours, and some-

times just for the comfort of being around your own people. There was always activity there and I kept hoping to find relatives or friends. And to my complete surprise, one day I actually found someone. In the middle of a cluster of people I suddenly saw my aunt and uncle, my mother's older sister and her husband. "Auntie, auntie!" I cried and then wept with joy when they saw me. I took them to our place and we managed to make room for them too. They wanted to know all about us, but when my aunt asked whether we had already eaten, we were silent. "All right," she said, "I have some food," and she prepared a meal. We ate eagerly and then immediately went to sleep.

Their presence gave us new confidence; we did not feel so lonely and abandoned anymore.

Next day we went again to the Judenrat, hoping perhaps we might see other relatives who had not yet made their appearance: my aunt and her two sons who had been saved at the hospital; my grandmother; and my mother's only brother. They should be coming any day, we thought. Suddenly, as we walked about among the people, I saw a woman, perhaps thirty-five years old, embrace my aunt crying out, "Jadzia!", her eyes full of tears. I had never seen the woman before.

But my aunt obviously knew her well and was now asking, "But what are you doing here, Renia? How did you get here?"

"You know my story, and my origins. You know my husband worked in the coal mines. Last week he was on the night shift. He had been telling me for a few months that his comrades there were giving him trouble, and I urged him not to get into a fight with them. But it seemed the more he gave in the more they harassed him until last night he could stand it no more, and he and one of the men began to quarrel. On the way home this man went to the Gestapo and informed them of my Jewish origin. A few minutes later a truck pulled up at our door and four Gestapo men, fully armed, jumped out and noisily burst in on us, yelling 'Dirty Jewess, trying to save yourself by marrying a Gentile.' 'But I converted to the Christian faith years ago,' I tried to explain. And they shouted, 'The Führer does not believe in such nonsense. If you were born a Jew, you are a Jew, and you're going to die. And now you have ten minutes to pack a bag for yourself and your children and come with us!' It was very early in the morning and bitter cold and my daughters were asleep. They didn't know anything and did not want to get up. And the four soldiers meanwhile kept shouting for me to hurry up. I was so upset and confused that I didn't know what to take or what to do. We were just leaving when my husband returned from work. He turned pale with rage. 'The black informer—I'll kill him, him and his family!' I begged him in Polish to be quiet and to think rationally how he might save us, and we would figure out later how best to avenge ourselves. My husband then turned to the Gestapo and asked where they were taking us. 'To the ghetto,' he replied, and here we are."

At that moment the younger daughter pulled at her mother's arm, complaining, "Mother, stop talking to these damned Jews!"

At this I jumped as though bitten by a snake. I was accustomed to hearing these insults, but—here in the ghetto! It was too much. Renia was embarrassed and flushed a deep red. "Quiet!" she commanded her daughter. "Watch your tongue!" But the atmosphere became heavy and unpleasant.

"Renia, my dear," said my aunt, "I can understand everything else—but why did you raise your own children to hate you and *your people? That I'll never understand. It's not only what she said, but the way she said it!"*

"You are quite right, Jadzia," Renia admitted. *"I am ashamed, but—it is the environment we lived in. My girls always suffered from the other children who used to say, 'Your mother is a Jew' so scornfully that they'd come home crying, asking me what this meant. Children can be very cruel, you know. I was afraid to tell them the truth and avoided giving them any kind of clear answer. So, to protect themselves, they became even more hostile toward Jews than their friends. I should have told them the whole truth when they were small."*

"If you had the courage to take the step you took, Renia, you should also have had the courage to tell your children the truth," said my aunt. And then she asked, *"And have you been happy? Or do you regret converting to Christianity?"*

"After so many years of deluding myself, and now being here in the ghetto—my feelings are rather mixed," Renia replied sadly.

"Come have tea with us this evening," said my aunt, *"and we'll have a good talk."*

"I'll be glad to—I need to talk with someone who is close to me."

After they had left I asked my aunt to tell me about the woman whose daughters dared to speak like that in the ghetto. My aunt answered, "Renia's story really begins about fifteen years ago, after she had left her home to go to university." She went on to explain that Renia had been born into a religious middle-class Jewish family. They were my aunt's neighbours, and the *two girls, being of the same age, were close friends. As a child Renia did not seem any different in character or personality from other Jewish girls, or even as a teenager. Her parents were religious but liberal, and since she was an excellent student, they wanted to give her a higher education. She was admitted to the university after graduating from secondary school with honours. Her family was very proud of her. Her father, a black-bearded Jew, used to go to synagogue every day and was proud of his Jewishness, while her mother observed the dietary laws strictly as prescribed. Renia's first year at the University of Warsaw was filled with excitement. She met a variety of young people and was introduced to a life she had not known at home. The studies, reading, and discussions broadened her mind and since her parents had provided her with money, she did not need to do outside work to support herself. They were not rich, but they bore the burden gladly because they were sure she would reap the benefits. "They took such great pride in her," my aunt said.*

On holidays Renia used to come home, and when she regaled her friends with stories of her exciting new life, they were quite envious, for they did not have such an opportunity to improve themselves.

On her way back to Warsaw on the express train she used to read, not paying any attention to what was going on around her. One day, however, a handsome young man, a student at her university, entered the car in which she was sitting. When he found she was a fellow student, he sat down to chat with her. Not shy by nature, he introduced himself and soon overcame her hesitation and began a friendly conversation. In the course of small talk and questions they discovered they were both from the same locality, and their interest in each other increased. By the time they arrived in Warsaw the foundation for a firm friendship had been established, and they decided to meet again.

So began their romance. There was nothing wrong with it, except that she was Jewish and he a devout Catholic. At first they ignored these differences. Being in love, they had more pressing things to think about. They tried to avoid appearing in public for fear of gossip, but later they stopped caring about it. By the time they accepted the reality of their situation it was too late, for they were deeply committed to each other. Finally, he proposed to her. At first she said no, because of their different faiths. But he had a solution: that she convert to his religion and thus become part of a "normal, healthy" nation, no longer one of a race of strangers. By assimilation, he assured her, the Jews could solve their problems, and she should serve as an example for others so that their future offspring would not have to suffer as others had. He did not insist, or pressure her. He simply suggested she think it over, quite sure her feelings would dictate her answer. And he was right. So in love was she that she could not sleep with the thought of losing him. Finally, she made her decision and, packing a bag, went home to tell her parents.

Her mother and father, as always, welcomed her with boundless love, but when they heard what she had come to tell them they thought she had gone mad. Even her brother and sister were shocked. Bedlam reigned in the house. They demanded she sever all contact with the Christian boy, that she not bring shame on her family, who had always been faithful to their religion. But nothing helped. Renia was in love and refused to give him up. She was ready, she announced, to make the sacrifice, willing to be converted to Christianity. They could not stop her. They cut off her allowance, and she returned to Warsaw to tell her lover what had happened.

Meanwhile, at the boy's home the consternation was no less extreme. "Marry a Jewish girl?" his father shouted. "Shame on you! Couldn't you find a Christian girl at the university? You bring shame on us. We are a respectable family; we gave you a chance to study and get ahead, so you wouldn't have to work in the mines like me. Is this how you repay us for our efforts?" The boy was ordered to cut off all contact with Renia and, when he refused, his allowance too was stopped.

They tried to continue studying on their own but couldn't keep it up. Alone, without family, friends, or money, they went to a priest and were married. They rented two rooms, and the young husband was forced to accept the only employment offered him, work in the mines. Life became dreary and hard—quite different from what they had imagined it would be. The husband often thought of the intellectual's career and status that had been within his grasp and was now lost forever, while Renia, pregnant, busy cleaning and cooking, often wondered, was it all worthwhile?

The rest I heard from Renia's own lips: "Today, here in the ghetto, I can tell you that after living for years among the Poles I have changed my mind. Their religion was foreign to me, their holidays I did not enjoy, and on Friday evenings my heart used to ache and my eyes fill with tears as I recalled my mother lighting the Sabbath candles. Life and drudgery. My husband worked very hard in the mines, and I found life dull. I tried to make friends with my neighbours but always felt myself a stranger among them. And so the years passed until the war started."

"On Christmas Eve, in 1940, my two daughters gave me a gold chain with a cross attached. This pleased me and I put it around my neck. But I heard my neighbours whisper, 'Look, she's wearing a cross!' and I felt stabbed to the quick. I felt persecuted. I avoided leaving the house so as not to see their looks and hear their nasty remarks. Then the terrible thing happened at my husband's work."

"Do you regret it all, Renia?"

"Well, to be truthful, my feelings are mixed. My husband has not rejected us. After work, he puts a Jewish identity band on his sleeve, and sneaks into the ghetto to see us. And when he leaves, we all wish him good luck. At least we are still alive. He brings us food and is planning our escape. He is loyal and doing his best for us...."

One evening, when Renia did not appear, we knew that their escape had succeeded and we were glad.

Chapter Twenty-Four

In December of 1942 Poland was shrouded in the snow of a very cold winter. Through the window one could see the snowflakes falling like white feathers and covering the ground, the trees and the roofs. It was much better in bed under the blankets, for of course we had no heat. Generally hunger would awaken us, but the knowledge that we didn't have enough to eat only made us hungrier. I was sitting in bed under the blanket when I was startled to note that my aunt was cutting the piece of bread we had into two, adding to one half some potatoes, a little sugar and some beans, and tying them up into a parcel.

"Do you intend to give our food to somebody?" I asked her, amazed.

"Yes," she answered quietly. "Get up, girls. It is Hanukkah today, and some members of the Hassidic organization, Matti, are in the ghetto to organize the sending of parcels to Germany for our boys who are hungry there. We too have a boy and girl in the camps there. They may be hungry. You are young, but one day you'll realize that it is our way to help one another, and we should be proud of it."

"But what kind of a name is that for an organization—Matti?"

"Matti is almost a legend now, to the Jews in the ghettos," she replied. "In Vienna, before the war, there lived a family who had a son considered to be a real genius. They were assimilated, but nevertheless he suffered at school for being Jewish. The youngsters abused and humiliated him but whenever he told his father about it, his father always said to pay no attention to them. One day the Rabbi of Gur arrived and a large crowd gathered around his house to welcome him. This boy, whose name was Mattityahu, or Matti, as the children called him, happened to pass that way and he inquired what all the commotion was about. When he was told, he decided on the spur of the moment to go inside and ask the great Rabbi to answer the many questions that preyed on his mind. His brief chat with the Rabbi so inspired him that he made up his mind to run away from home, go to Poland, and become one of the Rabbi's disciples at the Hassidic court of Gur. His father engaged some private detectives, and they found him and, by court order, brought him home. But on the way back he escaped. This made the father realize that his gifted son was not at all happy with the life his parents thought so good for him."

"When the war broke out, the parents were expelled from Vienna and sent to Poland. Here they met up with their son again and it was he who extended the necessary help, not only to them, but to many others. For he had organized a Hassidic group that was active in the ghettos and they named the organization 'Matti' after him."

The little parcel of food was ready and my aunt prepared to leave.

"Auntie," I begged, "please ask them whether there is any good news from other parts of Poland."

After she went out I thought to myself—today is Hanukkah. Everywhere in the world Jews are celebrating the occurrence *of a miracle two thousand years ago, when other enemies tried to wipe us out. Could not a miracle happen here and now? We had no candles to light, no gifts to distribute or receive, we were not singing Hanukkay songs—but we did get dressed and wait, perhaps for a word of good news on this holiday. But no miracles. Auntie returned in a gloomy mood.*

"What did you hear? Did the people have any news?" we wanted to know.

"Only that they murder us everywhere in Poland. They tell about resistance efforts staged by some religious Jews like Rabbi Shmuel Leiner, who moved to Voldova, near Lublin. He ordered his people to go into the forests and join the partisans, commanding them not to surrender alive to the killers. His order was carried from town to town and the Jews there rose up against the Germans, burned houses and shot at German patrols. But very few of them managed to reach the forests. Scores fell. Then the rabbi planned another breakthrough and escape, but someone informed the Gestapo and they went to arrest him. His servant pretended to be the rabbi and was shot dead on the spot. Later, when they learned that they had been deceived, they caught the rabbi and killed him after subjecting him to dreadful tortures. Yet his last words were 'Do not surrender!' And he was not the only one. Rabbi Zemelman of Pshtiz came to Warsaw, urged the people to rebel, and himself smuggled firearms into the ghetto from the Aryan side. Also Leib Shransky, one of the active Mizrahi members, joined the rebels in the Warsaw ghetto, and when caught by the Gestapo with weapons on him killed himself with a hand grenade."

There were more stories and details we already knew. In those days we spent our time ferreting out every possible bit of information. Now, dejected and in urgent need of some distraction, we went out into the streets. We would celebrate Hanukkah with a stroll in the ghetto, trying to forget.

When we returned some time later, one of our neighbours rushed to meet us, and cried, "How lucky you were out! Two policemen came looking for you. They'll come again. Better go and hide." My aunt ran off to the ghetto centre to see if, in fact, a round-up was in the process.

I was shocked to a standstill, but my mind raced. I could see Dr. Mengele and the experimental barrack, as I did every night in my dreams. What is left? I would rather make a run for it and get killed by a German bullet. For a second I wondered whether I should talk to my sister about how I felt. I thought—no. I'll wait until auntie gets back. I was again aware of the woman speaking. "What are you waiting for? Run! Run away!"

But I was not going to move. "No," I told her calmly. "We have no place to go. They may have received an order from Dreier to round up another shipment for Auschwitz. They'll find us. And we're too tired and weak to run much. We're staying, and may the end be quick." I didn't really care about anything except to be allowed a fast death.

My aunt returned quickly. The ghetto was calm. The police were not looking for anyone except, it seemed, the two of us.

Two hours later the two policemen came again with a note and asked for us by name. "Yes, here we are," I said, pointing to my sister and myself.

"You?" They glanced at each other in surprise. "Stand up!" They looked us up and down and seemed puzzled. "What's the matter?" I asked impatiently.

"There must be some mistake," one of them replied. "We have an order here to transfer you to the Dolek so you can be sent to work in a German camp. It is a direct order from Waldenburg, but there must be some mistake!"

Until that moment I had scarcely given a thought to the letter I'd written to my aunt, because, given our youth, it would be a miracle if we were actually admitted to her work camp. Now here was our miracle! Here was the gift sent us for Hanukkah! I could put out of my mind, at least for the present, the fear of having our skulls crushed, of being experimented on by Mengele and his staff, or having our skin torn off for use in plastic surgery, and all the other nightmarish victimizations of Jewish children. I was overcome by something close to elation and quickly packed our few things. Bidding our aunt and uncle goodbye, we followed the two policemen. At the ghetto gate I saw two boys, one who at the age of seven had been my "first love", and his older brother. When they saw that the policemen were leading us somewhere, they stopped, pale and trembling, and asked sympathetically, "Where are you being taken?"

"To the Dolek. We are being sent to Germany to work."

I could see they did not believe me. They were no doubt thinking that my imagination had run away with me. "Good luck!" they called after us, and we turned for a last look at them as we left the ghetto. A van stood waiting outside. We boarded it, followed by the policemen, and were driven to a huge building, all fenced in, with guards posted at the gate. We were brought to the commanding officer. The policemen saluted and said, "We have brought the two Jewesses demanded for work at Waldenburg Camp."

"All right," the German officer responded. "You may go back now."

We were taken to an office and when asked about our ages, added four years to them. They then took us to a hall lined with bunks, gave us supper, and sent us to bed. That night, for the first time in a long while, we slept quietly, without jumping up at the slightest sound. At five o'clock in the morning we heard shouted commands to get up, get dressed, be ready for a whistle, go to eat. Another whistle blew and we marched into another room where we were assigned to one of several groups, each identified by a number. We did not know what to expect. We waited half an hour. The commanding officer was there with a list of names in his hand. Now and then he began to pace back and forth nervously. Suddenly he roared, "Achtung! " and in came SS Obersturmführer Knoll. He was a tall, broad-shouldered man, carrying a briefcase, his uniform trim and covered with medals. The commanding officer of the Dolek stood at attention before him and then handed him the list of names and ages. "Here you have, sir, three hundred Jews demanded for work in the labour camps in Germany," he said and the two of them began to look us over very carefully. "Now," I thought, "this is it. This man will decide whether we are to live or die." They were checking each group thoroughly, looking everyone over individually, now and then taking a boy or girl out because he or she did not look fit, asking about ages and the state of health of each. Before they reached us I managed to whisper to my sister to behave calmly and to answer with confidence so as not to betray our real ages. "We have to be convincing! " I told her.

When they reached us, they stopped amazed. "What are these children doing here? " Knoll shouted. "They don't belong here! " But the officer extended a letter and read it to him.

Knowing Yiddish, I was able to make out most of the German. The letter said:

> SS Obersturmführer Knoll, Heil Hitler!
> Our plant needs two more workers. The camp I manage is run according to the Führer's orders. The prisoners' work is satisfactory and their behaviour good. We all do our best for the victory of the Third Reich. With the approval of the factory manager, each prisoner has the right to ask that her relatives join in the work of the camp. The first such request I have received is from Bronka Frischer, who asks for Chava and Rosa Gershonowitz. We need them to fulfill the production quota of our plant.
> With best wishes,
Heil Hitler!
>
> Mrs. Bittner,
Camp Commander

For a few minutes he stood thinking. Then leaning down to my sister, he asked her how old she was. She replied in German—again adding four years to her age. "What are you going to do in the factory? You are so small." She stood on tiptoe and said, "You see, that is how I'll stand and work. I'm strong and healthy, and I'll work as well as any of the others!"

Then he approached me and asked for my age. "And why are you going to the camp?"

"To work," I replied confidently.

A tense silence filled the hall. We knew our fate lay in his hands. He thought another moment and then gave his approval. We *breathed a sigh of relief. We were safe, at least for the time being.*

When the ordeal was over and we scattered, the Jewish orderly came over to us and said, "How lucky you are! It's hard to believe! I've just ordered the kitchen to give you extra food. Go to bed early, for you will be leaving very early in the morning for the labour camp in Germany."

That day we were given what seemed to be enormous quantities of food, and this improved our mood considerably. Immediately after supper we went to bed, relieved of the terror in which we had lived for the past two years. At least, we thought, although we'll be in a labour camp and have to work hard, we won't suffer so much and be afraid of every footstep. But it was not exactly as we pictured it.

Chapter Twenty-Five

The next morning at 4:30 the commanding officer strode in shouting, "Get up, get ready to travel. You will leave one hour from now!" I woke up. It was still dark and I wanted to sleep very much. But at once I remembered where I was and why, as did my sister. We leapt up, dressed, got into line, packed and waited for orders.

Then we were called to report for breakfast. After breakfast we lined up again for roll call. Then, together with a third girl, also bound for Waldenburg, we went out by threes. A young SS officer with rifle cocked escorted us. "Ready!" he shouted.

"Ready!" shouted the commanding officer of the Dolek, handing the documents to the SS man. We then realized he would be our escort and guard on our journey to Germany. We were not permitted to talk with him, only to ask a question at most, and we had to follow orders. We mastered this habit at once as though born to it. A moment later he turned and ordered us to march to the railroad station, while he followed us with his gun at the ready. I felt the urge to laugh and had to hide a smile with my hand. Whom was he guarding so earnestly? But he was in no laughing mood. He knew he had to escort us as prisoners. It was early in the day but the streets were already busy with people. I heard someone remark, "Look at those girls, so young and already criminals." As we went past her and she saw the numbers stenciled on our dresses she shrugged, "Ah, it's noth-

183

ing, they're only Jews." I heard similar remarks several times again before we reached the station.

We boarded a train which took us from Sosnowiec to Katowitz; here we waited for another that would take us further into Germany. As we waited I observed the travellers coming and going, listening as trains arrived and left, hearing the tumult and the noise going on about me. It had been a long time since I had been in the midst of the outside world, and it seemed to me there were two different planets residing in the same soil. These people travel in trains with dining cars and padded seats, not in cattle cars like our people. They are well-dressed and well-nourished. Happy. The children have mothers taking care of them, not a soldier with a gun. And yet they are no more human than we, created by the same Creator. Then why the difference so sharply drawn? It was obvious we lacked the loving care of a mother. We were two shabbily-dressed, skinny little girls with solemn, aged faces and not a trace of joy in our eyes, a mirror to the ghettos of our time.

We were put in a separate car, empty except for the three of us and our guard. We sat on two separate benches; the soldier on the bench opposite us. Throughout the trip, which took several hours, not five words were spoken. We gazed through the windows the whole trip. It was a beautiful sight—farmhouses and fields, dogs running free, snow-covered meadows and fine old trees. We approached a town. There were tall houses, many women and soldiers in the streets. The shops were open, but the largest crowds seemed to be at the kiosks where the newspapers were sold. People stole a look at the headlines and then went on their way. Most of the women seemed to be holding small children by the hand, yet they walked quickly. Now and then we could see a child start to cry, probably because he was tired, and his mother would pick him up and carry him in her arms.

"We have only a few more stations to go," the soldier suddenly announced and lapsed into silence. About an hour later he said, "At the next station we get off." We stood up, collected our few belongings and waited for the order to disembark.

At the station the soldier asked some passers-by for directions to the labour camp. After half an hour's walk we saw in the distance a wooden barrack with a fence surrounding it. Girls were walking around on the grounds. They waved to us from afar, and then most of them gathered at the gate to welcome us and to hear news from the outside world, particularly the ghettos. The most excited was, of course, my aunt, who still could scarcely believe that she had actually succeeded in bringing us to her camp. She was weeping helplessly. We reached the gate, the soldier stood at attention and then handed the papers and his three charges over to the directress. She took one look at us and turned pale. I doubt she heard a word of what the soldier was saying, for as she opened the gate I heard her cry, "Oh, what a scandal we're going to have! What have you done, Bronka!" as she turned to my aunt. "Why, they're mere children! They won't be able to work at a spinning machine with one hundred spools to be served. The head of the department will refuse to accept them and the manager will be furious. What are we going to do, and how am I going to explain their presence here?" Nervous and distressed, she paced back and forth, obviously not knowing what to do. The girls got together for a quick consultation—and decided to put us, for the next day or two anyway, in the kitchen. Two kitchen workers would cover for us in the factory. The camp directress was greatly relieved with this solution.

All the way to the camp I had been so happy at the prospect

of being free of anxiety at last—and here it was back again. The atmosphere worsened from one hour to the next; the mood of my aunt and the other girls deteriorated. I suspected that we were the cause. Maybe the Germans would send us back—or to Auschwitz.

Again there were nights when I could not sleep a wink. Again unrelenting fear. How I longed to be eighteen years old! At least to be like one of the girls. How I envied them!

However, after a few days had passed, they seemed to grow accustomed to our presence, and they even started to question us about life in the ghetto. Each girl would ask whether we had by any chance ever encountered her mother, or sister, or brother. "My sister lives right around the corner from you; did you ever see her?" asked one, while another said, "You may have met my mother." "Did you ever see my father, he is all alone now?" Some of their people we knew were no longer alive, and others we did not know at all. So we devised one answer to all the questions: "I'm sorry, we don't know them, we can only tell you the general situation inside the ghetto." Nor could we tell them much about the world situation. "The German press speaks only of their victories, and we hope that is not true. But one thing we can tell you girls. You should be happy with your lot. Don't you complain. Compared to the ghetto you are in a paradise here!"

Conditions at the Waldenburg camp were quite humane. The camp had been constructed around the factory and the whole area was surrounded by a fence with a locked gate, whose key was in the keeping of the camp directress alone. We lived in a long barrack which consisted of four rooms and a kitchen. Each room contained four double bunks, and each girl had one shelf in a cupboard. We worked at the factory eight hours a day spin-

ning thread that was shipped to other factories for the manufacture of blankets needed by the German army.

There were two reasons for the uncommonly good conditions at Waldenburg. We were but one hundred girls, and the Nazis, who expected the International Red Cross and other humanitarian organizations to demand inspection tours, kept it and a few other camps as models—showcases behind which they could conceal the atrocities of the bigger camps to which visitors would not be taken. The other reason was the camp directress, Mrs. Bittner. She was tall, with red-gold hair, and her face reflected her natural good nature and her innate respect for human values. An educated woman from an aristocratic German family, it was obvious she did not believe in Hitler's racial policies. But she took her job seriously and knew she could keep production at a high level if she provided her prisoners with decent working and living conditions. She fulfilled her duties scrupulously without resorting to the cruel methods used elsewhere. Even the SS officer responsible for the camp grasped the wisdom of her approach and refrained from applying harsher methods, helping Mrs. Bittner maintain her pride and satisfaction in doing a good job for the Führer. We still knew we were prisoners, yet the physical and spiritual circumstances were such that we could bear our lot. Once a month an inspector would come from the SS, either Obersturmführer Knoll or Lindner, and conduct an inspection tour.

Shortly after our arrival, we were presented to the head of the department. When he saw his new workers he flew into a rage, and Mrs. Bittner almost resigned her position on the spot. "What do you mean bringing me children?" he hurled at her. "This is not a kindergarten! We have to produce for our soldiers. It is cold on the battlefield, and they need the blankets we produce. They're fighting for us. It's the least we can do for them. We *need workers and not little girls."*

When he calmed down, however, he put us to work at a machine with eighty spools. He showed me how to tie a broken thread properly. I tried very hard to keep up with the other girls and to a certain extent succeeded. Every few minutes he would come over to observe how we were doing, and when he saw that we were not lagging behind, he stopped his constant vigil. I worked frantically at that demanding machine and thought to myself that the peace I had dreamed of was still far away.

The department head was a young Czech, a handsome young man with big blue eyes and the face of an angel. But he had the soul of a devil, a man of split personality. He was fanatically loyal to the Führer, but not ready to fight for his newly adopted Fatherland. He understood the dangers of being a dedicated Nazi. To avoid being sent to the front, which he knew was likely to cost him his life, he developed a conscientiousness that was worse than a German's. He had to elevate his job to heroic proportions and all day he ran like a crazy man from machine to machine, driving us mercilessly to produce the maximum, to prove how vital his role was to the victory of the Third Reich. I strained myself to the utmost, for I realized that my life depended on this Czech traitor, much as I despised him. Evidently he sensed my feelings toward him just by reading my expression, for he obviously hated me. I was afraid to look into his eyes, for they were the eyes of the devil himself. Over and over again he told me that my aunt had deceived Mrs. Bittner by persuading her to bring in children. Whenever he passed by me I went cold with fear, and if the threads happened at that moment not to be in perfect order, he would give me a look of such venomous hatred that I would tremble all over. I ran back and forth at my machine for eight hours a day non-stop, looking like a little bug in front of a huge giant. I concentrated all my energy and will on pleasing this cold, mean-hearted traitor, and at the end of the eight hours I was thoroughly worn out with the physical and emotional strain. My sister behaved the same way and the strain of it told on her too.

We were, as I have said, one hundred girls, mostly from Poland, a few from Czechoslovakia. Most of the girls were attractive, full of life, pretty as blossoms. Mornings, when the week's orderly shouted the order to get up, we would all jump from our bunks, dress quickly, wash, eat our breakfast and take our slice of bread and jam with us. Then we lined up for roll call and marched off to work, escorted by a guard.

At the factory each had her appointed place at which she worked all day. At five o'clock we again lined up in rows, marched back to the barracks, went through roll call, and were allowed to disperse. At that time, early in 1943, the first thing we did on our own time was to ask whether any mail had come for us. Cut off from the world as we were, our longing for letters knew no bounds. All during the hours we worked at the machines we kept hoping for a letter, for news of family and friends, and perhaps a word of affection and encouragement. A girl fortunate enough to receive some mail was radiant with joy, while those who were not, walked away dejectedly. The recipient of the letter would read and reread it hungrily and then read it aloud for the rest of the girls. She allowed herself her own private happiness and then shared it with the rest of us. The reply would be written that same evening, the girl putting down her own little problems, enjoying the act of discussing them with a loved one. My sister and I decided that we too ought to write to tell our relatives of our safe arrival at the camp.

While those responsible for the camp were far from pleased with our presence there, the girls seemed very happy to have us with them. We reminded them of the little brothers and sisters they'd had at home, in the days that now seemed so far away, when mothers and fathers were still alive. Seeing us brought memories flooding into their minds, and they would tell us about their homes and families prior to the war. They showered us with attention and affection, as if we were the siblings they so loved and missed. And we, in turn, enjoyed them as we would a family of older sisters. They devoted a great deal of their time to us, taught us to spell correctly, told us about things we did not know and, best of all, told us stories.

These girls opened up new horizons to us. Experience had made us all too familiar with Hitler's racial "science" and the lowest reaches of human behaviour. But otherwise, we were two ignorant little girls with little formal education. I had only three grades of school and my sister even less. We knew hardly anything of history, geography and other school subjects. From early childhood I had always been interested in history, and I now begged the girls to tell me various chapters in the history of Poland, especially about the liberation under the leadership of Pilsudsky and the population's delirious joy at their newly won freedom. At that moment in my life it was particularly exhilarating to hear this story, precisely what I was constantly dreaming of for ourselves.

Every evening after work we would lie down for a rest and then, after dinner, we would sit on the benches and talk about anything that came into our minds, different ones among us taking the lead. These turned into discussions, opinions, memories and experiences. And for me, a brand new subject turned up—love. Love at school, first love, the first kiss. A whole romantic world was revealed to my sister and I, for whom these were as yet only abstract notions. We listened raptly to all this without talking. For us these were tales of a thousand-and-one-nights. What we knew, the stories we could tell, were sad and tragic and, in any event, no news to any of these girls, so we merely sat and listened, glad to forget for a while the realities around us. In those hours a sense of hope stole into our hearts—perhaps a ray of light would yet brighten our future!

Then came sleep and all too soon the shout, "Get up!" And in the winter how much I wanted to sleep a little more, if only five minutes longer, and kept my eyes shut as if all the shouting did not concern me. But hands returned to shake me, "Get up, it's late, you won't be on time!" and scold me into hurrying. And then came the flash of memory of where I was; I mustn't, I of all people, cause the slightest trouble or draw undue attention to myself. I was too young to be here and was allowed to stay only out of extraordinary kindness. Here was no different than anywhere else, Jewish children had no priorities on life. Electrified, I would leap off my bunk, rush to wash in the icy water, gulp my breakfast, hurry in to place in line, and so to work.

Time crawled interminably in the factory. Small wonder, too, for it was forced labour, done without zeal, only out of fear. Our natural distaste for what we were doing was greatly increased by the knowledge that our work was helping our enemies in the very act of destroying our people. We all kept watching the clock, and as the hour of five drew near, many girls began to whisper that they hoped they would find mail waiting for them. Finally the door would open, the second shift would enter, and the girls would come and replace us at the machines. Again the lines and the roll call, and the redeeming "Disperse!"

We ran for the mail. Most of the girls were disappointed; letters were arriving less and less frequently now. As for us, it was our aunt who was the recipient of letters. I cannot remember all of them, but three of them have remained engraved in my memory. For some reason the Germans did not concern themselves with censoring our mail; perhaps, again, because they had so much faith in the efficiency of their extermination system. At any rate we, and those writing to us, expressed ourselves freely. At first the mere sight of our family's name on an envelope made me happy. Although I knew they would never be signed "Your loving Mother", they came from close relatives we loved; we still had a grandmother, aunts, cousins, and of course, a father. Their handwriting was familiar to me, but it was puzzling when one day a letter in a strange hand arrived:

Dear Mrs. Frischer,
It will no doubt surprise you to receive a letter from someone you do not even know. Although I am not related to you, our common lot has linked us all together. I take the liberty of writing to you because, as the saying goes, a drowning man seizes at a straw. From my cousin, who is in the same camp with you, I learned that you succeeded in bringing your two nieces into the camp. I remained in the ghetto with my two daughters whose ages are twelve and fourteen. My husband was sent to a labour camp and the rest of my family to Auschwitz. I have money and valuables and am ready to give you anything if only you will bring my daughters and me into your camp. You are our last hope. Please do everything possible to save us from certain death . . . .

The next letter was in a different vein but included a similar request:

Dear Mrs. Frischer,
Your having succeeded in bringing your nieces into the camp with you has turned your name into a legend among us in the ghetto. You keep hope alive in many a heart, and many will doubtless appeal to you for help. I realize your camp cannot be considered a permanently safe refuge, but it is definitely the best place for us at this moment. Many will probably offer you fortunes, but I unfortunately have nothing. All I have left in the world is my fourteen-year-old daughter, a lovely girl who wants very much to go on living. I too would like to survive and see the day when our torturers are defeated, and then take revenge. I am not a harsh person by nature; in fact, all my life I have been considered easy-going and kind, but . . .
We are sitting on a volcano that at any moment will erupt . . . . If you cannot take us both, then do everything to take my daughter.

And I remember a third letter, again asking for refuge, from a woman who also had only one daughter left, promising that "if I shall stay alive, I shall be like a sister to you and serve you in any way possible, and look after you. Please, please try . . . ."

Every day my aunt received letters like these, as though we were in Switzerland on a vacation. These letters from the ghetto could only make us weep, for we knew their end was near and we could do nothing to save them. We ourselves were far from secure and fully realized our precarious position. We had created such a tumult that at any moment one of the department heads might write a letter of complaint to Eichmann's office in Berlin. At each inspection we trembled from the first moment to the last, and our aunt never knew where to place us in the line—at the head, in the middle, at the end—to draw the least *attention and thus avoid being told we did not belong here.*

Then Mrs. Bittner was dismissed from the position of camp directress, and another woman was appointed to take her place. The change worried us, for we liked and trusted Mrs. Bittner. She had proven herself a gentle woman again and again. She had joined the Nazi party only out of necessity, that was obvious. Before leaving the camp she said more than once, half in jest, "Girls, if the Russians come, I hope you will defend me and my husband." We assured her in all sincerity that we would, for we were very grateful to her. My sister and I also felt quite guilty, for perhaps it was because of us that she was fired. We were sad to see her go and yet impatient to see the new directress.

She was an altogether different type of woman, much younger, better looking, and well dressed. Not nearly so well educated as her predecessor, she was very strict: with her an order was an order, to be obeyed implicitly without any question. She was uncompromising in her demands for order and discipline, but she did not change the routine already established. It was her ambition to have everything run smoothly. She was very proud when at the monthly inspections she presented her report which stated the factory had no problems, that our work was satisfactory, all was clean and tidy, and there was no serious illness. She took full credit for the felicitous state of affairs, and the SS officer gave her the satisfaction of agreeing with her. In Mrs. Bittner's case, he had genuinely respected the woman for her character; with this lady, he was agreeable because of the evening the two spent together. We always knew in advance when he was due to come because she would dress more carefully, have her hair done and use perfume. He would come in the afternoon, look the camp over and read the report, and then stay with her through the night. This was very lucky for us—

what the previous directress had achieved by means of her personality, the present one obtained in bed. There was a Czech girl among us who had been a seamstress at home. She now volunteered to sew new dresses or alter the lady's old ones, and her offer was accepted eagerly. This rebounded to the benefit of the whole camp, because having someone to dress up for made her more amiable to us, and thus we did not suffer from the change in administration.

Chapter Twenty-Six

Our girls were not only attractive but also intelligent. Each one did her work with the same feelings of hatred and resentment as I did, for the same reasons, but nevertheless did it well out of a sense of collective responsibility. If one of us broke any of the rules, all were punished. The bitterness that filled our hearts found expression in the curses that we voiced when we left the factory at the end of the day's work. "May everything we produced be burned up!", or, "May the freight trains carrying it be blown up on the way!" There was no point in sabotaging the work, for they could easily replace us and have us put to death.

My aunt, deluged with letters begging for help, answered as many as she could, explaining sadly that she could not fill their requests because there was no need in the camp for more workers, no room to accommodate any more inmates, and another under-age scandal would bring certain disaster on the entire camp.

In later stages, when additional workers were needed, the Nazis brought in Christian boys from Czechoslovakia, France and Italy. They were housed in a building across from our camp, also on the factory's grounds, but they were not prisoners. They were, however, obliged to live in the building and not venture far from it, returning always at a specified hour in the evening and reporting every day for work. Their arrival brought changes into our daily life. To begin with, it was pleasant to see friendly faces and to hear some news from the outside world. We were anxious to learn what was going on at the eastern and western fronts—were there victories or defeats? What was the general state of mind? We were seeking a source of information in the hope that some day the war would finally come to an end. Until their coming, our only contacts with the outside were the local German women, non-prisoners who worked with us. By this time we could understand and speak German fairly well, and we listened carefully to their conversations. But they complained only of the cruel bombings of Germany by the Allies, which maimed and killed many of their people. We listened to their criticism, taut with the effort of keeping silent. The German soldiers, according to these women, were always careful to aim "only at military targets". One of our girls could not keep quiet any longer and she asked a complaining woman, "Do you know what happened to our parents, brothers, sisters? How they departed this world?" The woman refused to believe it. We were angry at this girl for speaking up, for had the woman gone to the management to report her, she and all of us would have suffered.

The German women worked hard too, but they did so out of love, for victory and the Fatherland. Their blindness amazed us, for some of them were educated and many intelligent. Yet all of them gave blind allegiance to what the press and radio told them. We realized that the Germans, with this kind of public support, would fight to the last soldier, as if they were under a spell. What chance could we possibly have, then, against their Führer and his sadistic plans for us? What if they win the war, we trembled, and—what if they should lose! If they lost the war would it make any difference to us? The hatred was so deeply ingrained. How often had we heard, "Win or lose, we'll finish you!"

We had no answers to the questions that were in our minds, and we did not talk about these things to one another. But each and every girl among us thought only of being free. That was what we wanted, and we sought eagerly for any sign, any indication, that might point to its possibility. Hence our wish to get acquainted with the new boys. But all talk or contact with them was strictly forbidden. Our attractive girls drew their attention, of course, and they tried to find a way for clandestine meetings. They too wanted to exchange a few words, but there was the language difficulty—only one girl knew English and a few knew Czech; all the rest spoke only Polish or German. The boys on the other hand spoke only their native tongues. We were therefore forced to cling to our routine, which at that time was overcast by news that yet another transport had been shipped to Auschwitz. Now most of the girls who still had parents were orphans like ourselves.

In the midst of this fresh sorrow we received a letter in a familiar hand. It was from my aunt Regina, the mother of the two cousins we adored so much. We asked to have it read aloud so we might know its contents at once.

> My dearest sister and nieces,
> Our small ghetto has been liquidated and we have been shipped to Shrodule. I sold everything I had left to buy food to take with me. On the appointed day I was brought with my sons to Shrodule, and near the Judenrat I met our sister Jadzia and was overjoyed to see her. After the first greetings I asked her about our sister Esther's two daughters, for, knowing that they had been left alone, I considered it my duty to take them and care for them to the best of my ability. When she told me that you, Bronka, had managed to bring them to your

camp, my mood improved further still. I had not dared to hope for such wonderful surprises in the ghetto.

Dearest sister, try to bring me and my boys to your camp too. I will dress them as girls and let their hair grow. When I told them what I was writing to you, they asked me to add that they were both strong and big and able to work. Just to look in their eyes shows how much they want to live, and here in the ghetto every minute is fraught with danger. They are well developed beyond their ages, both mentally and physically, and they understand what is going on and always listen to the talk of grownups. When I look at them I cannot help but cry very often. Both are really handsome boys. They have become so attached to me since Haim was taken away to the camp. If you succeeded in bringing Esther's girls there, I do believe you will find a way to save us from immediate annihilation too. But you must act at once, for tomorrow may be to late.

It occurs to me that perhaps your directress may be able to hide us at the home of relatives in some distant place. I am ready to give her all I have and do whatever work she assigns me, even the very hardest, to save my children. Is there some hope for us?

With our love,
Regina and the children

After reading this letter, my aunt wept without pause along with us. We did not even go to eat our meal when our day's work was done. Each of us knew very well that the desperate hope this letter expressed was only an illusion and could not *be fulfilled. Now would come the most difficult part, the inevitably negative response. It was inconceivable bringing boys into the girls' camp, they were even younger than my sister and I. Smuggling them elsewhere was out of the question for us. The woman who had exerted herself especially for our sake had been dismissed, and we had no contact with her any more, while her successor was an active member of the Nazi party and the commander's mistress. We could not trust her, and any attempt to discuss with her our relatives' escape would in all probability prove fatal. We did not talk about it that evening for our hearts were too filled with pain. The irony of it, that a labour camp had become a refuge!*

We went to bed without saying a word. Only when a few days had passed did I ask auntie what she had written them. Had she explained the situation precisely as it was, so that she would not suspect us of not trying hard enough? She must know how dear her children were to us. We too were more than willing to work extra hours every day in order to save them. But we could do nothing! I lamented again that I had not been born at a different time—how could we bear such grief and sorrow! I could not know that this was a paradise compared to what was awaiting me in the next eighteen months. I sensed from my aunt's state of mind the letter was ready, so in the evening I asked her to read it to us. This is what she showed me—she could not read it for weeping:

> *My dear and beloved sister and nephews,*
> *Writing you is the most difficult thing that has fallen to my lot, for the reply must be negative. You place all your hopes in me, but do you really think for a single moment that you can fool such a team of murderers into taking boys for girls? They would never get past the Dolek. I understand you well, sister, and*

your desperate pleas, even though they are impossible for me to fulfill. I wept the whole night after receiving your letter. But we have no time for emotions; we must be practical, face reality, look for a way out.

The second plan you suggested is also out of the question. Our first directress has been dismissed and the new one is very strict, she does not know me and will not want to do anything for my sake. I've spent sleepless nights trying to think of some other way I might be able to help you, but there is none. Regina darling, have you no other possibilities there? I remember you had many business connections before the war with monasteries and were personally acquainted with many monks and nuns and other church people. It seems to me that the only way is for you to entrust a monastery with the care of your children, to hide them from the Nazis. Then, if you cannot be with them, I will try to bring you here alone. I can think of no other way, though I have tried hard. Act as quickly as you possibly can and let me know. I need not add how much I love you all, especially the children. I wish you success in all your efforts.

With deepest love,
Bronka

We mailed the letter and began to count the days—two weeks passed without word. Distressed and bewildered, we were afraid we had added three more victims to the enormous total. Or were they still in the ghetto? Would she write us her answer? We wrote again begging for an immediate reply. When it came at last, I did not have to ask—my aunt's face told its contents. I took it and read:

Dear sister and nieces,

You may easily imagine our disappointment, all our hopes shattered by your negative reply. Did you actually weigh your advice before suggesting that I turn my sons over to strangers? You have no heart and no feeling. It is obvious you have never been a mother. I shall never be parted from them; it must be all of us or none. We will not go separate ways. No monastery wants to take all three of us despite all my offers to give them everything I have. They won't even take the boys alone, even if I were willing to part from them. We must therefore endure our fate together. This advice I did not need.

Forgive me, sister, I am so confused. I may have demanded the impossible of you, but in my despair I thought, who knows, perhaps you may work a miracle for us as you did in the case of Esther's daughters. I am happy they at least have been spared immediate danger. I do not know how many more letters we will be able to exchange, so try to keep them well and take care of yourself so that some remnant of our large family will endure. May you win freedom and happiness for yourselves and all those things a human being deserves to have. The years of my life have been good and full of meaning. We realize how lovely our life is only when we have to leave it. The world is filled with light and sunshine, but it is not intended for all of us, evidently. One madman has turned it topsy-turvy and robbed us of our rights as human beings. I can only send you my love and kisses and best wishes.

Your loving
Regina

Reading this letter I felt the full force of tragedy, the tragedy of the Jews as a people and of Jews as individuals in this century. There was no going home in peace after the play has ended. I wondered whether people would believe what we went through, even if they knew about it. These were my thoughts as I read the letter, the next to last we received. The last was from my grandmother.

> Beloved daughter and granddaughters,
> It has been years since I wrote a letter; I always asked my son to write for me. But this time I don't know whether it will be possible for him to express what is in my heart. And I feel I must express the bitter feelings that weigh on me. This introduction will not help you guess what is on my mind, but if I tell you a story first, you will know.
>
> A few days ago Mrs. Klein came to visit me and found me in a very bad mood, as if any other were possible under the circumstances. She thought, however, that it was because of purely personal reasons, and, trying to console me, she said, "Darling, you must reconcile yourself to the tragedy that befell Esther. You know we all face the same danger and can at any moment be sent off to the crematorium at Auschwitz. Esther was lucky." I did not know what she was talking about, so I asked, "What disaster befell my daughter?" She became confused and tried to change the subject but I insisted and everything was revealed to me.
>
> Can you imagine my shock? I did not know where to turn or what to do. I decided to light a candle in her memory and could not be sure whether according to

the Law I may not sit the seven days of mourning for her. I was very bitter toward you. Did you have the right to deny me my right to accompany my daughter to her eternal rest? Does anyone have the right to do this to a mother? I am trying to forgive but doubt if I'll ever be able to. I realize how hard it was for you to put on such an act for my benefit and that you did it for my sake, to keep this pain from me at a time when we had so much suffering already, but this is the greatest wrong that has ever been done me in all my life.

Dear children, I am now in a mood in which it does not matter what my fate will be, and in any event we can change nothing. I think this will be my last letter to you. Be strong, and daughter, look after my granddaughters. May God watch over you and give you the physical and spiritual strength to overcome all the difficulties you must face. May you live to be strong and healthy and free Jewish girls, and continue the line of our Jewish people. For throughout thousands of years no tyrant has been able to wipe us out. This murderer and all his henchmen will fail. I don't think I shall live to witness their defeat, but I hope you will. Being young and healthy God will bless you and keep you from evil, for "the People of Israel are alive." This has always been our motto and it continues now. And you will be part of the People. I pray you may see the fall of the Third Reich and the deserved end of all enemies of decent people, and their trial for the inhuman crimes they have committed. It is so hard for me to take leave of you; the stains on the paper are my tears. Goodbye, my beloved ones—I embrace and kiss you from afar. Be strong in the face of all the conditions that may yet be forced on you, and may it be God's will that you overcome them all, for it is your sacred duty to go on living. Again, goodbye, and God bless you.

With my love,
Your mother and grandmother.

Grandmother's letter was, in fact, the last, and not only for us; nobody received any more mail. From August, 1943, all contact with the outside world ceased. We knew the reason—Sosnowiec had been declared Judenrein. All the girls in our camp were now orphans. We were all in mourning, apathetic, negligent of our appearance. We talked little, moving only in nervous jerks. Our spirit was quite broken.

The keener, more alert girls noticed these signs of spiritual breakdown and were determined to do something about it—otherwise we were doomed. One of them, Bella Windling, offered a concrete suggestion: "Girls, the Nazis want to destroy us all. A small part of us is still alive, thanks to the work. But now our behaviour is such that we are helping our enemies achieve their goal. We must not let this continue; we must be strong and survive. I have an idea—I'll write a play, and we will perform it. We'll try to forget the bitter reality for at least one evening. What do you say? Everyone will take part in one way or another, and it will take our minds off our troubles for a bit."

Her idea was accepted enthusiastically, and she began that very evening to write her play, titled "The Two Thousandth Century", which she finished in a short time. Eager as we were to forget things for a while, it was not totally possible, for the play was related to the reality that oppressed us. But we put a lot of energy into the preparations for the performance. The gifted girls were given parts to play, while others were chosen to make the necessary arrangements—a room that could be made into a theatre, installation of seats, a curtain made out of sheets and blankets, and costumes. Everyone became so involved that each of us contributed some clothes, a sheet, or whatever was needed to help make our play a success. The Czech seamstress worked now also in the evenings so that all might be ready. We made rapid progress, the actresses never too tired to study their lines and rehearse. The rest of us, who were supposed to be the audience, were not allowed to attend the rehearsals, so as not to destroy the surprise effect. Finally the date for the performance was fixed, and I began to count the days in eager anticipation.

It was such a change from the heavy routine we had been following for so long that I could hardly wait to experience it. For three years we had seen neither theatre or cinema, and for a short while we were in an exalted mood. We were more relaxed, our youthful exuberance made a re-appearance. We had a new theme to occupy our minds; we discovered new talents and beautiful voices among us; we composed songs for solos and chorus, and even some humourous scenes about our own weaknesses and foibles and the changes that occurred after the arrival of the foreign boys in the camp. Ever since their arrival, each girl spent a few precious minutes every morning combing her hair, and all changed clothes more frequently and tried to look their best. The feminine instincts of the normal young girl were awakened by the sight of nice-looking young men who had no murderous intentions, and the urge to make friends with them was so strong that despite regulations and the lack of a common language, ways were found—eyes, face, hands helped express what tongue could not. The French and Italian boys sometimes threw kisses. The boys as a whole were far from indifferent to the girls. Notes were exchanged in secret, and the boys passed parcels of food to us, often delights we had not tasted in years. We always shared everything. Some of the girls even received letters suggesting escape plans, which were all very gently rejected out of a sense of responsibility to the rest of us. On spring and summer evenings after work, the Italians and some of the French boys would sit on the window sills and sing serenades until nightfall, while we would stay outdoors and listen with pleasure. I must admit most of our girls had some success with the boys, but not my sister and I—we were too young, nobody paid any attention. It disturbed me, and even though I knew our age was the cause, I kept looking in the mirror to see whether I wasn't too ugly. I knew the serenades were not meant for me, yet I enjoyed them as much as anyone, and in the morning I spent a few minutes on my hair, a real sacrifice since I always wanted a little more sleep—but it was all quite fun. Yet I never managed to get a letter from one of the boys; neither did my sister. All of this sentimental experience was good fodder for our show and for sketches in the humourous "newspaper" prepared in conjunction with it.

The anticipated day finally arrived. To make it specially festive, we all put on the very best clothes we had. When the show began, the atmosphere was tense; excitement was in the air. The room was still, the curtains parted, and Bella, our playwright, made the introductions.

Some of the skits moved us deeply, even to the point of tears. But things took a lighter turn when the humorous pieces started. The satire and good-natured fun provoked gales of laughter. Much of the criticism was aimed point-blank at one or another of us, and I was pleased to be the butt of some of the jokes. If I was not successful in "love", it was good to know that I had traits that some people found entertaining or worthy of attention. When the show came to an end we got to our feet and sang the Hebrew anthem "Hatikva", which means "The Hope". A few words, spoken to mark the conclusion of this very success-

ful evening, expressed the hope that we would someday see a show in a free atmosphere, without barbed wire fences encircling the theatre and guards poised at the entrance gate.

Although we knew what fate befell our families, our uplifted spirits made us hope that we might yet meet some of them, someday, somewhere. We simply would not imagine life without a mother and father, sister or brother, or someone close who would love us and be loved by us. Deep in our hearts we all believed that once liberated we would find some of our relatives still alive. I always felt deeply grateful that we three were together, my sister, my aunt and I; we were in fact the only ones in the camp to be so lucky. The show released a whole chain of pent-up dreams and emotions—dreams of freedom, love, relatives, life without roll calls and commands and that detestable work.

Next morning, however, we were back in the reality of our dreary prison life, getting up quickly, dressing, eating our poor breakfast hastily, and marching off to the drudgery of the factory.

For me Tuesday was the best day of the whole week. If I was working on the morning shift, I would be taken on a special and interesting trip which broke up the monotony of our days. I could then see people, especially the children, who did not as yet know what was going on in the world and who were still quite innocent.

Our destination was a special slaughter-house where horsemeat was distributed for the camps. We had a wooden cart; two girls pulled it from the front as though they were horses and a third one pushed from the back. Each of us was glad to take the part of the horse so, to be fair, the turns were rotated with three dif-

ferent girls for every week—with the exception of my sister and me. At the request of the directress, we were added as extras for every such trip, so we always went along without robbing any other girl of her turn.

The first time I went I looked at everything we passed in Waldenburg: the attractive houses, clean streets, the mothers walking along with little children. And there we were, girls from the spinning mill, drawing the cart like horses, with an armed guard to watch over us. The number on our clothes had to be clearly visible, and that made us conspicuous and directed the attention of the passers-by to us. We were often in a milling crowd and I could hear their remarks. Once I was within earshot of a mother and her little boy, and could hear their entire conversation. I remember it vividly. He asked her, "Who are those girls?" and she replied, "Prisoners, my son."

"What was their crime?" he asked further.

"They are Jews."

"But I don't understand you," the boy said. "Lately you answer all my questions in a way I can't understand. I asked you what crime did they commit? Why are they prisoners? Did they steal or kill or refuse to work?"

"No, son, when you get older you will read "Mein Kampf", which the Führer wrote and then you will understand. They are enemies of the Third Reich."

"Why?"

"Because the Führer says so. He says they must be destroyed."

"But why? What did that little girl do, the one in the blue dress?"

"Nothing."

"Then why has she got a number and why is she a prisoner?"

"You don't understand," the mother became angry, "so stop asking questions."

"And you answer my questions, and don't tell me stories the way you do lately. I have to understand, so when you explain you shouldn't say things that are not clear."

The rest I could not hear as they walked away.

In another case the girl was about nine. I heard her ask, "Mother, we always see these girls with a guard, pulling that cart—who are they?"

"They are Jewesses," the mother answered.

"Why are they being guarded? Did they commit sabotage? Or refuse to work for our victory?"

"No. They are our enemies."

"They are? Why?"

"That is what the Führer says and whatever he says is right. We must obey him without asking any questions or arguing."

I heard such questions and such answers over and over again. One boy stands out in my mind. He seemed about twelve. I overheard him ask his mother, "Why did the Führer write that the Jews are our enemies and we must destroy them? He accused them of all kinds of things. I remember some years ago most of our neighbours were Jews and I used to play with their children. They were my best friends, and their parents were nice too. When I think about it now I never saw them show any signs of the things they are accused of in "Mein Kampf". Why does the Führer want to kill them?"

"Son," this mother replied, "I do not know the answers to your questions. Ask the leader of your youth movement. He knows." I wondered, "How could such a highly civilized people have become such automatons?"

In the meantime we arrived at the slaughter-house to pick up our meat rations. What a different atmosphere we found there! The girls' hearts began to beat rapidly. There was a British prisoner-of-war camp nearby and the prisoners came to the slaughterhouse for the same reason we did. They were young men, all good-looking, all English. We stared at them to see what English gentlemen looked like in real life, having read and heard about them so often. They were very friendly and certainly not indifferent to our girls. My sister and I had already grown accustomed to having no attention paid us by the opposite sex, yet during the time we spent there we too admired their looks and energy. I was sorry for them, for they were in a Nazi prisoner-of-war camp. But I surmised that, as soldiers, their conditions must be much better than ours. In the first place, they showed no signs of fear and talked with our girls quite freely. However, we could not understand them. All we could make out were the few words of German they had managed to pick up, such as: I love you, come sleep with me, you are very pretty, how charming, etc. We laughed at this not only because of what they said, but the way they said it. It showed they were trying especially hard.

But their accents were peculiar and made us giggle. They amused us and, what is more important, gave us the welcome feeling that there were still people who found us attractive as girls and wished to kiss and love us. For all we could expect from a German male was curses and beatings or worse. That is why every girl was eager for her turn to be the horse and pull the cart, putting on her best clothes for the occasion and trying to make herself look pretty. We were only sorry that but one of us could speak English.

I remember that once an English boy who knew German well was among the group in the slaughter-house. He began to ask us who we were, where we were from, why we were here, whether he could send a letter through us to his family. He was trying to find a contact with the outside. I'm not sure he really believed what we told him. He just kept repeating, "It cannot be—it's impossible. Are you sure?" He seemed to look upon what we said as a fantastic horror tale. And who can blame him!

When we returned to our camp we would be swamped with questions: "What kind of boys are they? Do they speak German? Did they tell you their names? What do they look like? Are they nice?" As we found out later, the English boys as well were asked questions about our girls when they got back to their camp. They told their friends all they knew except for one thing, it seems—namely, what kind of camp we were in.

One day when we had finished work and darkness was setting in, we lay down to rest on our bunks, each one absorbed in her own thoughts. The rooms were still. The afternoon shift had not yet returned from work. Suddenly the girls in one of the rooms heard a moan from behind the window. They listened, not sure what they had actually heard. "I hear a sigh from under the window," cried one. "So do I," called another. It was already dark *outside. They listened for a long time. The moans started again. One of the girls looked out the window and saw a young man lying on the ground groaning. Quickly they went out to him, but he spoke only English and they could not make out what he was trying to say. Meanwhile the word was passed around—"an Englishman"—and the entire camp was in turmoil. We were excited and frightened. One of the girls demanded that we stop the noise, worried that we might attract the attention of the guards. We looked for the only girl who could speak English, the Czech girl, Fella. To avoid rousing anyone's suspicion, she went to him all alone and asked who he was and what he wanted. He told her he was a prisoner-of-war, twenty-four years old, fed up with prison life. He wanted to go back to fight. As our camp was in their vicinity, he added, and we were always friendly, he decided to run away from his camp and ask for our help. He was a bit bruised and cut, probably from climbing over our barbed wire fence. Fella then explained to him what kind of camp we were in, that we lived under guard, one hundred girls without a single man, without any connections whatsoever with the outside world and no possibility of leaving the camp except to go to and from work under guard. "All we can do is wish you luck and commend you for your pluck," she said.*

Then she called the girl who served as our nurse and they attended to his bruises. He was a very handsome man and we were all, by now, in a state of high excitement. Someone said, "He must be hungry", and everyone was eager to give him whatever rations they had, to keep him going until he reached a safer place. Fella explained to him how dangerous it was for him here—he was terribly conspicuous amongst a hundred women. She urged him to get away quickly, our guards were always on the alert.

It was late but we could not sleep. We prayed for him, knowing full well his life was in danger. He chose his freedom in a very hard way. He was young, ambitious, and his natural feelings would not let him sit still. We realized then that the English boys could not have known what our camp was like if they hoped to find a road to freedom through us. Had this fellow really counted on our help? We didn't know.

Next morning we listened attentively to the German workers as they talked, for they were our only source of information. They mentioned nothing about the young man. We hoped he had succeeded in escaping to freedom. But when we returned to the barracks after our day's work, we suddenly heard shouts of "Open up!" We could see four Gestapo men, accompanied by police dogs sniffing the ground and leaping at the gate to our camp. They circled the camp, but the key was in the hands of the directress, and she had gone to eat her supper. Our hearts pounded, thinking at once of the English boy, and we stood waiting, some of us outside and some within, to see what would happen. From afar we could see the directress running, flushed with excitement. "What is wrong, gentlemen? What do you want?" she asked the Gestapo breathlessly. "Is something out of order?"

"Did you see a prisoner-of-war around, an Englishman?" they asked her.

"You don't suppose I would open the gate to let such a one in here, do you? How could he be here when the key is still in my possession?" They laughed at her naive reply, but since she made the statement in all seriousness, they realized that she did not think there was any other way of entering her grounds. They asked her to unlock the gate and they came in. I hid in a corner. Since my first experience with the Gestapo dogs I had been terrified of them. They searched in all the rooms, looked us over and questioned us about the Englishman. We revealed nothing. Then they whispered among themselves and left. Only *when they had gone did the full shock of the experience hit us.*

Many of us had diarrhea from sheer nervousness and fright, and the queue for the washroom was a long one. We knew that, if caught, the prisoner would be subjected to the most horrible tortures, of which the Gestapo had a large stock. And if he broke down and admitted being with us for a while, we too would suffer beatings, hunger, extra hours of work. The optimists among us assured themselves and the rest of us that he wouldn't be caught, and even if he were, he'd never give us away. But these problems weighed on us all through the night. Every sound jolted us upright in our bunks. The next day there was again no news of the prisoner from the German women.

The day came to a close and still there was no news of him. Everything was quiet. We never did find out whether he managed to escape or was caught. If he is alive somewhere in England, I wish him well and would dearly love to know what happened to him and how he fared.

Chapter Twenty-Seven

The year 1943 was drawing to a close. One month was left before 1944. Eichmann's office now functioned most decisively and without the slightest restraint. Our camp directress informed us one morning that instructions had come to turn all camps into concentration camps and, inasmuch as ours was not equipped for such a change, we would have to be transferred to another, when she did not know. No more labour camps, only concentration camps. We discussed this ominous news amongst ourselves, trying to ferret out the reasons. Obviously, we decided, the Germans no longer felt the need of a "showcase" camp; the world's passive acceptance had made its mark. Possibly the Russian advance contributed to their reasoning too. But regardless of the logic behind it, such peace and security as we had here was destroyed at one stroke. Our chances were still better than in the ghetto, but fear was now a permanent fixture.

I was working on the second shift and was about to go to the factory when the directress suddenly arrived and told us to remain as we were. The SS Obersturmführer then came in and passed through all the rooms. He ordered us all to undress completely and line up in rows of five so he could pass between us. My aunt did not know where to put us: at the beginning of the line, the end, together or separately. She feared we might be "selected", as it was termed, when the weak, the sick and otherwise less fit were pulled out of line and sent to the nearest gas chamber.

We undressed and lined up in front of him feeling shame and deep humiliation. My sister and I were very much under-developed, even for our true ages, but we were mentally quick; we joined a woman who was very short and stood with her between us. Slowly he passed between the rows. Somehow he did not notice us, and gave an order to dress. Never in all the months of my imprisonment in the Nazi camp was I so happy to go to work as on that day.

A week later we were ordered to pack. Each girl had one bag. We were all very worried, though we tried to cheer one another up. Our slogan was not to break down, to keep our spirits high, and not help them implement their Final Solution. We felt that it was our duty as Jews, for the sake of future generations, and this gave us the courage we needed.

A day before we left Waldenburg a large number of heavily armed SS men appeared. Next morning at five o'clock we were awakened, ordered to put our kit bags on our backs and line up outside. It was December. Snow was falling, and the cold was sharp. The armed soldiers surrounded us, and we were ordered to march to the railroad station. Special carriages were waiting there for us. We boarded the train and it began to move. Not being familiar with the geography of Germany, we could not guess where we were going. After many hours of travel, we reached a station at which we were ordered off. They counted us to make sure no one was missing and marched us off to the concentration camp in Groben, near Gross Rosen. We were exhausted from the long trip by cattle car and were marched for another hour before we saw from afar many barrack buildings fenced in by barbed wire. We tried to spy out the girls there, for their appearance would tell us a great deal, but we saw none. Hungry, dirty, and weary, we went through the gate. The Jewish camp "officer" received us and then we stood in the dusk waiting.

Suddenly the German directress appeared as the officer shouted, "Attention!" Then, addressing herself to the German woman, she said, "These are the hundred girls from the Waldenburg camp."

The Nazi woman was young, dressed in a Nazi uniform, and very formal and exacting. She asked a few questions, demanding that our answers be brief and to the point. She was not there to chat or provide information to prisoners. She assigned us to rooms, twenty-four girls to a room. And at once we became acquainted with our new circumstances. The first girl we met was asked whether there was a crematorium here. She answered, "Here—no, but nearby in the central Gross Rosen camp there is one." "Who are our guards?" "German SS and Ukrainian Volksdeutsche," she answered meaningfully. The latter were collaborators who were worse than the Nazis. They would shoot even without orders to do so. It was enough to just walk past one of them for him to kill you on whim. They excelled in their jobs, their cruelty exceeding anything the Germans practised.

The food at the camp was poor, and the girls went about hungry, working twelve hours a day, from six to six. The most minor deviance in behaviour drew severe punishment, at times collectively. If, God forbid, one of us was sick for more than a week or had something contagious, a black van would come and take her off to a crematorium. We fresh arrivals heard the conditions now facing us, went to wash up and swallow our bit of soup, and then were permitted to go to sleep. That same day we were assigned to our jobs, half to the day shift and half to the night shift. I was to work days. At 4:30 in the morning I heard a whistle. This was the signal to get up, wash, and eat soup. At 5:30 another whistle commanded us to line up outside in the dark. Each girl took a piece of bread with her to the factory. We were received by the foreman, a middle-aged German who looked us over and assigned us to specific jobs. We were in an immense weaving plant filled with many sections and rows of machines arranged for assembly line production. It was so dense with fumes and soot that we were scarcely able to see one another. The German workers were given special food vouchers for eggs, meat, and fats in return for eight hours work in the plant because, when inhaled for an extensive period of time, the soot was injurious to the lungs and often caused tuberculosis. But for us, we worked twelve hours daily on niggardly rations.

I sensed the extraordinary hostility immediately. We were not treated like human beings, but like dogs, our pleas answered with a grunt: "You're not people, you're dirty Jews and you've no right to complain." My job was to push a cart filled with soaked flax on rails to a huge oven that stood at one side, and as it went along the rails, the flax dried; that's all I did, all day, without a break. On the first day the foreman led me to the cart and said, "You will work here." My companion, also assigned to this job, was a Russian prisoner. I looked at him, and he smiled, "We will work together. My name is Ivan."

I told him my name was Chava, which he pronounced Eva, and added, "But I don't speak Russian."

"What language do you speak?"

"Polish."

"Good," he approved. "I worked with Poles who fled to the Soviet Union when the Nazis attacked and I learned to speak Polish from them."

Every now and then he would speak some Russian words too, but I had no trouble understanding him. After a while I said to him, "Ivan, it's nice to work with a friend."

"I feel the same way, Eva. I'm only surprised he put you here, because the Russians are not usually allowed to come in contact with you girls."

"Well, you can understand why the foreman made an exception in my case."

"Yes," he agreed, and we both laughed. Then he added, "But he was wrong, Eva. If his intention was to keep me away from a girl who would make the working day more pleasant and arouse my feelings as a man, he failed. You are much more important to me than a full-grown woman; you remind me of my own daughter I left behind in Russia. I haven't seen my Katya for two long years."

"Where are you from, Ivan?"

"I come from a little village near Kiev. My wife Caterina, my two sons and my daughter still live there."

"And your parents?"

"Oh, they live in Moscow. But tell me, Eva, you are so young, why did they take you for such hard work?"

"It's lucky for me that I'm here," I told him. "Others of my age did not even have the chance to get here. I am a Jew, Ivan."

"I know," he assured me. "In all the countries they conquer

they draft the young people to replace the millions of men they have mobilized into their army. But what kind of luck is it for you to be in a concentration camp and have to work so hard? I don't understand. Where are your parents? And your family?"

"Dead—except my father, and I don't know where he is," I explained. "Except for a very few, all the Jews were sent to the camps in Auschwitz, Treblinka, Majdanek and other places. They were killed in gas chambers and their bodies burned in crematoria."

He looked at me for a long moment, then asked, "Are you all right, Eva? Are you sick? Is the work too much for you?"

"Ivan," I said, looking straight into his eyes, "I am not mad or hysterical. It is not sick imagination on my part but the awful truth. There is not a single Jew left in the whole section where I was born. The few survivors are like me, those who succeeded in escaping either to labour camps or to Russia."

"Do you mean to tell me," he gasped, "that they destroyed children and infants that way? It's not possible!" he nearly screamed.

"Yes, and not only in Poland but in all the occupied countries."

"It cannot be—it cannot be!" he cried, repeating himself in Russian.

"Ivan, you are a prisoner-of-war, and yet you are being forced to work. In our previous camp we saw English prisoners-of-war, and they were not forced to work."

"That's true. According to the law they have no right to make us work, but when an officer we have among us dared to ask the German manager about this, he got two slaps on the face as an answer. Russia is not a signatory to the Geneva Convention, and it does not therefore apply to us. Russians, Jews, and dogs have no rights."

"Well then, Ivan, you and I belong to the same family and we are equal," I told him. He laughed, and added, "The minute I saw you I felt a tremendous yearning for my family, especially my daughter. I love them so and I'm happy that I'll be able to talk to you about my Katya. She is tall like you and has green eyes and long hair. Caterina, my wife, used to tie her hair back with two ribbons every day before she went to school. She was a good pupil, she liked reading and used to ask so many questions on almost any subject. Sometimes I didn't know how to answer and felt embarrassed. But I was proud of my little Katya, that one day she would be an educated person." Sighing deeply, he asked, "Do you suppose I'll ever see them again?"

"Of course you will, Ivan," I assured him. "The Nazis are fighting the Red Army and not the civilians. In the villages there can't be much danger of bombs. You must believe that and keep up your morale. One day the war will be over." He nodded sceptically, and we fell silent.

The German foreman never spoke to me but merely pointed where he wanted me to go as though I were deaf and dumb. It was heartwarming by contrast to have an opportunity now and then in the twelve-hour day to exchange a few words with someone like Ivan. Yet I felt that my strength was diminishing day by day.

A few months passed. It was almost the middle of 1944. One

day I came as usual to work and Ivan came too. But he was unusually pale and looked upset. "What's happened, Ivan?" I asked him.

"Friends of mine who were also taken prisoner have come here," he answered.

"What's the news? What did they tell you?"

"The Red Army is victorious and is advancing westward, and Russia is freeing itself little by little from the Nazis."

"But this is good news, so why are you so sad?"

"Yes," he replied, "but the retreating Germans are very cruel to the civilian population wherever they pass. There are many who have died of hunger, cold, wounds . . . ."

I listened sympathetically, but told him, "You see, Ivan, again history proves that you cannot win security and victory for your own people on the bodies of others . . . ."

"What do you mean, Eva?" He was puzzled.

"Look, Ivan, I have nothing against the Russian people, but I hate Stalin and his henchmen. Hitler's philosophy and his plans were no secret; Stalin knew them well. Still, he entered into a treaty with Hitler and did not care that by doing so, he was sanctioning the extermination of millions of Jews and others. I am only sorry to hear that the Russian people are suffering."

"The people always pay for the leaders' mistakes."

"Does anyone give help to the Russian people?" I asked, re-

calling that no one came to our aid.

"Oh, yes, Mrs. Churchill has been at the head of a special fund for the benefit of the Russian people since 1941 and everyone is trying to help. She issued effective appeals," he said, "and many people responded generously." His newly arrived friends had told him about it.

I was moved again to ask the eternal WHY? Why are the Jews a race apart? Was I perhaps simply too young, too mentally immature, to understand the reasons?

I ventured to ask Ivan, "You are older than I am, you could be my father, so tell me—how is it that when the Nazis killed millions of Jews, nobody came to our rescue? They knew what was happening. Churchill himself declared that the killing of Jews was part of the Nazi plan to rule the world, and yet nothing was done to stop it. Ivan . . . do you know why?"

"I can only tell you, Eva, that Stalin's pact with the Nazis was wrong. But I can promise you one thing . . . we are winning. All your people who survive, they can count on Russian help. Our ideology is social justice, to help those who suffer and are underprivileged. We'll protect all those people and care for them. The Russians will be your benefactors . . . they will champion injustice. After all have not the Nazis declared that Russians and Jews are one and the same . . ."

"Well," I responded, "it is good to know that you still believe in honesty and justice. I lost my faith in them as a child."

"I know everybody has disappointed you, but please, Eva, don't lose faith in the Russian people," Ivan insisted. "If I live, I'll prove it to you."

"You and your friends are people of goodwill, because you suffer as we do, but your Government? . . . Well, if we live, we'll see."

About two weeks later Ivan came to work beaming with happiness, which made me ask whether he had heard some good news. He said, "I'll confide in you because you are my good friend and I can trust you. We have just heard that the Red Army is advancing rapidly, they are very close, and we figure that very soon we shall be liberated. But some of us have decided to take an active part in the victory."

"You mean escape?"

"Yes," he whispered, "but be careful lest we are overheard."

"Ivan," I urged, "I know you are all experienced soldiers and you won't pay any attention to my advice, but you are wrong to do this. Do you have contact with an underground that could help you?"

"Here in Germany? No, of course not."

"Then listen to me, Ivan. I wish I could convince you. I don't know exactly where we are, but since we travelled for many hours from Waldenburg, it must be somewhere in Central Germany. Here you don't see men of your age out of uniform; so even if you get civilian clothes somehow, you will attract immediate suspicion. You'll have to watch out not only for men, but women and children too. They will suspect you and inform the Gestapo. I don't see how you can possibly succeed without help from the outside. You can't get away very far. They'll start chasing you with their dogs and set the whole vicinity searching for you. You can't imagine what will await you if the

Gestapo catches you. Our boys and girls used to carry poison in case they should be caught. What is more, they will punish not only you but all your friends as well, even those who remain behind. They will hang your officers and starve your men to death. Don't you care about them? Don't you feel responsible toward your own people?"

He listened attentively, his face becoming more and more serious as I spoke. Then he said quietly, "Thank you, Eva. I must admit we did not take all that into consideration. We just decided to risk our own lives." Then he agreed to discuss it again with his friends.

He failed to come to work for five days. They have escaped, I thought, and I prayed for his safety. But he returned smiling and announced, "Well, did you think I ran away? No, I was sick, that is all. We discussed the things you said and decided you were right."

"I really am right, you know. At least we've denied the Nazi sadists their satisfaction. And if one day you find a good way out, don't forget us . . . ."

All the victories being chalked up by the Allies and the Red Army did not, for the time being, bring the slightest change into our daily lives. The exhausting work, poor food and constant strain drained away our mental and physical resources. Then one day on our way to work we encountered a group of girls whose complexions were bizarre, a kind of yellowish-red. We began to ask them who they were and where they came from. It transpired that they were in the same district as us. "Why are all of you that weird colour?" "It's the work; we're in the dyeing plant. We don't last more than six months with this dye . . . As soon as one of us dies, she is replaced by another."

We did not ask any more questions.

Next day we met a group of men all in tatters. They were emaciated and weak, looking like musselmen. They'd been on the road several days, they said; they were being transferred away from the liberating armies. Anyone unable to go on was shot on the spot; the road was filled with corpses. We threw our bread rations to them but we could see that some were so weak that they could not stoop to pick them up, and they were probably shot soon after.

A few days later we saw a cattle train filled to overflowing with Jews. They had been crowded in so tightly that there was not enough air for all of them to breathe, and while some died of hunger and thirst, many died of asphyxiation. Seeing this, such a fury overcame me that I could not weep but only felt my heart being torn to bits. The inner tumult evidently showed on my face, for Ivan asked what had happened to make me look so bad.

"Oh, Ivan, I hate Stalin—I hate Churchill—I hate Roosevelt—But most of all I hate my own people who, through all the centuries our blood has flowed, didn't manage to create a state for us where such things couldn't happen!"

"You are full of hate, Eva. Don't you love anything at all?"

"No, I love only those who suffer with me. I'm too tired! I'm worn out with starving and working so hard. I'm tired of being afraid to be sick lest the black van comes and hauls me away. I'm tired of being terrified of the guards, and I'm tired of seeing my friends suffer. I am fifteen but look twelve. I think like a forty-year-old and I feel like an old woman of seventy. I doubt we'll ever be free!"

"Oh, my little Eva, how broken you are! And you are always telling me, 'Ivan, we must hold on!'"

"But, Ivan, I really am tired of trying anymore. It is now the fifth year of it. You are men, and Russians, and you have your military life in common and your country behind you. But we are women and girls without experience, without a nation to support us. Your chances are far greater than ours for getting free some day. Ivan, promise me just one thing, that you will work for justice and fight against hate and that you will tell about the Jews' miseries and convince people that no man can turn his back on it. Promise me that, Ivan!"

"There is no one who could tell your story to your people except you yourself, Eva. Not me. You must hold on whatever happens so that you will do it."

"If I live . . . ," I muttered. "I won't rest until I tell it all . . . ." We were on the night shift. It was past midnight. "In five hours you'll go get some rest and then you'll feel better," he consoled me.

"Don't be silly, Ivan. After twelve hours of hard work I can look forward only to rebukes at best from the directress, or to punishments for wrongdoing."

"What, for instance?" he wanted to know.

"For staying in the lavatory for more than a couple of minutes, for talking to a Russian prisoner, for idling for a moment during work hours. Even if everything is all right, we can't go to our room until after roll call. Before you close your eyes, it seems, the whistle gets you up again to prepare for inspection and march off to work. Sometimes we don't sleep more than a few hours."

Ivan listened but did not reply. It was clear that his conditions as a prisoner-of-war were much better, though he too had hardly enough to eat.

It was around two o'clock in the morning and I went to see the exact time. On the way the foreman saw me and shouted, "You"—he used the German "du", which is very impolite—"come here!" Trembling, I approached. "Come with me," he ordered and I followed him to another workshop. "You will work here, at this machine. Mrs. Hildenberg is tired and you will help her."

The German woman looked at me and remarked kindly, "You are so pale and you look very tired. Are you sick?" At once I was on guard. Her solicitous remark might lead to talk in the German employees' mess room about my being underage and weak and—to my end. In this sudden moment of danger my mind worked fast and I said, "No, Mrs. Hildenberg, I'm not really pale. It's only the light in here that makes me seem pale, and I'm not a bit tired. You know, the mere thought that I am working for the victory of the Third Reich gives me so much energy and will to work that I scarcely feel the hours and the effort." She was amazed by my passionate speech and, being a really decent woman, did not dream that a youngster would be capable of saying one thing and thinking another. Gently she said, "Eva, I'm going to leave a sandwich for you at the other end of the machine. Take it and go eat it in the lavatory so nobody will notice because we're not allowed to do this." I thanked her and, taking the little parcel unobtrusively, I went to the lavatory. Five years had passed since I had eaten such a good sandwich, with sausage and fat on it. My eyes brightened and my mood improved considerably. I took my bread ration and ran with it to Ivan. "Take it and eat it and tonight both you and I will not feel hungry!"

"No, Eva," he replied, "you take my bread ration. I saved it for you after I saw what a bad state you were in. I thought it might be the hunger and the bread might make you feel better."

"But I'm not hungry. I was given a sandwich and I'm not a bit hungry, and in any case, that wasn't the reason for the way I felt. Now hurry up and take it. I have to run back to my work."

Next day, however, I told him the whole story, about how miserable I felt for having declared myself eager to work for a German victory, and about the sandwich I was given. "You shouldn't have taken the food from her," said Ivan.

"But why not?"

"Because her husband may be among those who murder our brothers."

"I don't agree with you, Ivan. Her husband may be a murderer or he may be just a soldier at the front, but she showed clearly that she is a woman with a heart. It is the guilty who have to be punished, and as long as we do not have the facts we cannot judge."

During the first year in the concentration camp I was more than once in deep despair, but Ivan too was frequently in a bad mood. For a man who had fought at the front, it was humiliating to be treated as a common criminal and he was full of rage and frustration. We used to console and encourage each other. He always talked to me as if I were his daughter, and that seemed to comfort him.

More and more often now, news seeped through that the Germans were losing the war. Much as this gladdened us, it also reminded us of the frequent threats the Nazis made, "Win or lose, you we will certainly take care of! If we have to leave we shall finish you off first." I liked to ask Ivan whether he thought we had any chance at all, for he would answer, "Eva, the Red Army will destroy them before they have time to do anything to you, I assure you." I suspected he himself did not believe in what he was saying and wanted just to give me courage; still I loved to hear it. And then he would say, "I am just waiting to meet my friends. First of all, we'll destroy the fence around your camp, and then we'll liberate you, and I'll say— 'Here is your freedom'. That will be the happiest moment of my life!" I listened with rapt attention. "What a lovely plan!" We might as well have been planning a trip to the moon, so far-fetched and fantastic it sounded.

In the camp the atmosphere was ever gloomy. Each person's individual struggle for existence dominated everything. We were too drained and worn out, all of us. We had changed completely during our imprisonment. Like the inmates of the other concentration camps, most of us had lost the ability to know right from wrong. We became like animals living by instinct; we had ceased to feel sympathy, pity, we had lost the ability to mourn. We felt abandoned. We knew what the Nazis meant by their Final Solution, and we did not doubt that they would carry it out at the last moment.

Chapter Twenty-Eight

The war raged on, at all levels and fronts, and we were more miserable than ever. A ray of brightness came from one little girl among us, from Poland. She was very gifted and wrote many poems and short stories. Unfortunately, she did not live to see the day of liberation. I always loved to hear her read her own poems and stories, and whenever there was a free moment, I would ask her to read. She wrote only about the life we were experiencing or her memories of home. I cannot recall verbatim any of her pieces, although the substance of many I remember well. Her bunk was filled with pieces of paper on which she had scribbled something when it came into her mind. Her big brown eyes were sorrowful, not only for herself, but for all humanity. She wrote in the simplest language, without literary pretensions, but purely and chastely, as if the world had just been created and she were marveling at its contours. So deeply involved was she in her writing that she seemed sometimes to forget altogether about the war and the annihilation which threatened us. But from time to time, she would suddenly become conscious of it all and, like the rest of us, sink into abject despair.

Two of her poems I remember in particular. Let me try to convey what impressed me most in them; to give just a glimpse into this beautiful soul, that hardly caused any harm to anybody at any time. Her name was Pola.

THE MOTHER

The mothers sighed heavily, writhing with birth pains,
One cried aloud, the other was still.
And then a cry and an end to the suffering
A child is born—said the old midwife.
Great was the joy, lovely the baby,
All rushed to see her, this gift of a girl,
Innocent creature, angelically pure,
Looking about with her big, brown eyes
Unknowing of the good and evil
In the world, involving her destiny,
Unknowing of what to expect in the future,
And just demanding to eat; to eat
And breathe the air endowed to her.
Until she grows, and opens her eyes
And sees around just deceit and misery,
Blood and terror, the evil conquering.
Then she cries again: God, Oh, God,
Could not I be born in some other age!

WHY

In a village small a girl was growing,
Happy her heart full of love,
Love of mother, father, all.

Swinging and running and jumping rope,
Growing up with a wish to learn,
Reading, writing, drawing nature's beauty.

Not so, thought others, shattering her dream.
"You have no right! You belong to kingdom come!"
Cried the soldier in the polished uniform.
"But why? Why?" cried the little girl.

Chapter Twenty-Nine

No change, no break, no rest marked our days. Sometimes when I lay down I thought to myself resolutely: tomorrow I'll say I'm sick and have one day's rest. But then a small voice within me would say to me, "No, dear, you must not be ill. The work is what keeps you alive." I went under the blanket without any illusions and could only pray that some day soon it might be better.

In the factory, the Germans' state of mind was deteriorating day to day, while secretly ours was improving. And yet physically we were growing weaker all the time. Not a day passed without some news of the Allies' advance. Suddenly came a new order: prepare for transfer! Where? Nobody seemed to know.

It was December, 1944. The winter was very harsh and our clothes, especially our shoes, were torn. We were given wooden clogs. This time we had nothing to pack. All signs pointed to a hasty evacuation of our camp as the armies of the Allies were approaching rapidly.

Early in the morning we dressed and were ready when the whistle blew: line up outside by fives! The SS guards, fully armed and surrounding us on all sides, were ready to shoot down anyone who faltered on the march.

Such a march had its precedents. The road was strewn with

bodies, casualties of the groups that had gone before us. Conditions had so inured us to human suffering that not one of us shed a tear. The thought uppermost in each girl's mind was only not to become yet another frozen body on the road. The wooden clogs we wore made such a clatter that we could be heard for miles around. Twice a day we were stopped and ordered to excrete as though we were dogs, and once a day we were given some water.

At the end of a day's march we were led into stables for the night and locked in, and there we lay down to sleep, grateful to be still alive. When we asked where we were going or how far, we got no answer. At the end of three days we reached a railroad station and were shoved into cattle cars. The number of cars was insufficient and the congestion was terrifying. Suddenly we heard an air raid alarm. The Nazis quickly locked the doors and ran away to shelters. We heard the bombs exploding but were not afraid, positive the pilots would not hurt us—they knew who were in the cars! We laughed and rejoiced at the sound of the bombs.

Once daily the train stopped and we were given a piece of bread and some water. That was all our nourishment. We also had to stop a number of times for aerial bombardments and alarms. After travelling several days we reached hell-on-earth, the death-camp of Bergen-Belsen. SS men were waiting for us, and we were left in the efficient care of the world's greatest sadists. Again we were stood in rows and were counted, and again marched off. A gate was unlocked and immediately locked behind us, and we were in an immense forest. More gates were unlocked and locked and we passed through a succession of these until we came to a building with chimneys. This we were sure was the end. We had heard so much about the shower-rooms where gas poured out instead of water that we felt this must be it. There were girls like ourselves working in the building and we asked them where they were taking us. "To bathe," they replied, which, of course, we did not believe. All the girls were afraid to go in first, and we stood motionless. But I was so exhausted from the horrible march and train trip that I begged my aunt, "Please, let's go and get it over with. We won't change their decision anyway. If this is the end, let's go first . . . :" We undressed and turned on the taps—and suddenly water gushed from them! Delirious, we washed ourselves and put on the clothes the camp provided along with a black blanket, a wooden spoon and a bowl for each prisoner. We were then led into our block.

It was an oblong building, painted red, with a number on it. Many buildings of this type were there, with a barbed-wire fence around them and guards posted between each one. Our movements were restricted to this compound. The place was completely barren and empty except for others with our common fate, Jewish girls from various European countries who had been brought here from other camps. Their appearance proclaimed who were veterans of Bergen-Belsen and who were new arrivals. The new ones still looked human, but the old-timers were like living corpses, literally skin and bones, the eyes popping out of fear. Walking skeletons, the proverbial musselmen. We began to search for relatives and acquaintances among them. One of our girls found her sister there. We surrounded her and asked, "Tell us, how is it here?"

"There is nothing to tell; we have to hold on."

"How is the food?"

"Twice a day we get soup made of korpiele. That's all."

"How long can we hold on in our weakened state before we too look like musselmen?" we asked.

"Who knows! Before that happens perhaps we'll be liberated."

In the evening we were given the bit of "soup", water with korpiele in it and no salt. When I finished it, I felt as if I'd had nothing in my stomach, and still I had to run to the lavatory. It began to grow dark and we prepared to lie down on the floor in our clothes, covering ourselves with the black blankets. We were pressed together like sardines in a can over the whole floor, except for a narrow passage in the middle. One person's head faced the next person's feet. That night there were more girls than usual, so some even slept in the passageway. Anyone who has passed a night in Bergen-Belsen will agree that hell must be a paradise in comparison. It was impossible to sleep. Compressed as we were, we had to sleep with our feet and legs drawn up. Cramps invariably set in and when we tried to stretch our legs a bit it immediately set up howls from those on whom our feet rested—"Take your feet off my face, I can't carry you. I haven't got the strength!" In our physical condition the weight of another, no matter how thin or slight, was too heavy to bear. Others cried, "You're strangling me!" when their neighbour's feet and legs twined about their necks. All night girls had to get up and go to the lavatory; the soup they had eaten went right through them. This provoked further shouts and screams. Exasperated, some of the girls would answer, "But I have to go. Do you want me to pee on you? I can't help it." And others, the old-timers, would get up to shake their blankets free of the lice you could never get rid of—and remove their clothes, and shake them. They put them on again, and the process was soon repeated. And, of course, this was accompanied with more stomps on faces, necks and stomachs, and more angry shouts and screams. This was how a night went in Bergen-Belsen.

Every morning some were found dead. The head of our block would survey the scene to see who had died and order two girls to carry the bodies outside. A pile of corpses could be seen each morning next to each of the barracks. During the day a group of men, prisoners like ourselves, would come in a van to collect them. As the crematorium could not burn all the dead at once, another method was also used. They arranged a layer of wood, poured gasoline on it, laid down a row of bodies, topped these with another layer of wood and bodies, set fire to the pile, and then started all over again. These pyres burned all day and night. All we could see from the windows were heaps of burning bodies giving off their special nauseating stench.

Every morning I would shake my blanket and my clothes and take my place in the line for washing up. There were only two taps of ice cold water and two lavatories for a whole barracks filled with dozens of girls. It took hours to get to my turn at one, and then came the wait for the other. After that the soup, and if I was lucky I'd find a corner and lie down to sleep. All day I'd think about that corner in the hope of keeping it for the night, but I could not stay there all the time and guard it for myself. So, as a rule, someone else grabbed it and I had to lie in the middle of the crowded floor, kicked and trampled on in the helpless, miserable mass. Whenever one of us stretched her legs and heard no complaint from her neighbour, she could be sure that girl would never cry out again. The one who survived then had a better night . . . . These conditions turned us into animals; a neighbour's death was reported without any grief, without any emotion whatsoever. I too soon became one of the "night walkers" because of the lice—we lived in the same clothes day and night. I could not sleep for scratching; my body was covered with scratch-marks. Like the rest, I was trying to *shake my clothes clean, getting up in the middle of the night to wash my body and some of my clothes, spending much of the next day watching them as they dried.*

In two months' time we lost so much weight that we were completely transformed. To make matters even worse, a typhus epidemic broke out in the camp. One of the first to succumb was my sister. Her fever was raging, and all she could have was a drink of cold water, nothing whatever to eat. The mortality rate was so high that the place began to be roomy. Even then, most of us could not sleep due to fever, lice, and hunger. We were simply starving to death.

In February a new transport arrived. We approached them as quickly as we could, asking, "Where are you from?"

"We are Jews from Holland," they told us.

We looked at them—they still had their luggage! "What is the latest news?"

"There are rumours the war will end very soon," they informed us. They were exceptionally lovely people, and we soon found a common language. As my sister's condition had deteriorated, I appealed to the Dutch girls, saying, "I'm not asking for anything for myself, but my sister is so sick, could you spare a bit of food for her?"

"Here," a middle-aged woman offered, "I have some sugar. Take it for her." And she burst into tears.

"No, not all of it," I objected, "give me just a little. The rest keep for yourself."

But she refused. "I don't need it, and she does," she insisted.

I thanked her with all my heart and hurried to my aunt. We collected some sticks and, starting a little fire, boiled some water, adding sugar to it. Auntie fed this to my sister with a spoon, and immediately we saw an improvement in her condition.

One night, a week later, a Dutch girl was lying beside me. Tortured by the lice and hunger, I could not sleep. She turned to me and asked for water. I took her cup and went to fill it. She drank it down at one gulp and begged for more. I noted how her eyes were gleaming; she is burning with fever, I thought, and brought her another cup of water. She drank it and lay down, carefully placing a little package by her head. Later, when we had to huddle close, I noticed that in it was a piece of stale bread. My senses reeled at the sight. I had not seen bread for weeks. A fierce inner struggle now raged within me: "Does a hungry person have the right to take the bread of someone else? If I take it, I shall not eat it alone, but give some to my sister and that might save her."

I fought my overpowering impulse. In the end I concluded that—No!—even though circumstances had indeed changed my personality considerably, they had not destroyed my conscience. I would not touch her bread even if I died of hunger. It would save neither me nor my sister. The girl was obviously sick with typhus; in a few days her fever would go down, and she would begin to improve. She would need her bit of bread then; it might save her. And if she died, I would always feel guilty, thinking perhaps it was from lack of the bread I had stolen . . . . I did not touch the bread. But I did not sleep either, for I sat up to guard it so that no other girls would snatch it away. "She is asleep, poor girl," I thought, "the fever is making her sleep in spite of all the noise and commotion. In the morning when everyone was up, she was still sleeping, so I shook her, calling, "Get up, get up!" until my aunt came over and said, "What are you doing—can't you see she is dead?" Only then did I take her bread and give it to my sister, and helped carry her body outside.

February passed, and then it was March. The epidemic took a heavy toll, with the girls dying one after another. In the meantime we noticed a larger number of German soldiers moving among the barracks. When we concentrated on them, we realized they were technicians connecting electrical wires to the blocks. We watched them through the door. Yes, they were joining the wires between our block and the adjoining one, and the one after that. We understood. We had no chance of surviving. They intended to blow up the whole camp before the arrival of the liberating troops. We were not surprised. It was inconceivable that they would leave this monstrous proof of their crimes for all the world to see. Upon seeing the electric wire, I sat down in a corner, covered myself with the blanket, and mused bitterly on my fate—after six years of such suffering, I am to meet the same end as the others, while they had the privilege of preceding me. Then I thought: in books I'd read, the greatest criminal sentenced to die is always given a last request. Mine would be: first, to sit just once again at a table and eat all I wanted and drink hot sweet tea. Second, to bathe with soap and sleep just once again in a clean bed. And third, to go into a lavatory and sit there as long as I like without being disturbed.

Some cries outside wakened me to reality. "Come see, some new ones are here!" We stood fascinated. These were healthy, fat women. I'd forgotten such people existed. They did not look as though they had suffered much; any one of them weighed as much as five of us put together. In a moment we would know; they were being led to our barrack. We ran to meet them, asking in Yiddish who they were. This was the international tongue in which Jews from all over Europe were able to communicate. But they replied haughtily, "We don't understand."

"What language do you speak?"

"Polish."

We looked at them in astonishment. They seemed like creatures from another planet, all of them with lovely complexions. "Where are you ladies from—from which ghetto or camp?" we asked further, in Polish this time.

They tossed their heads in disdain. "We are not Jews. We are insurgents from Warsaw, our capital. We got caught!" Unlike the pleasant, courteous Dutch newcomers, these were not women we would want to encourage and so we left. I had thought when I saw them with their luggage that perhaps I might get something for my sister to eat, since her condition was critical. Complications had developed following her bout with typhus: sores in her mouth and an eye infection. But it was obviously useless to hope for anything from them. When night came, they took up a section of the floor, declaring it their own, and did not mix with us at all. They tried to stay apart as a group. This was the first time we had encountered people, doomed to share the same fate, who behaved in this manner. We did not protest. It was no special honour to lie on that dirty floor next to one of them, or elsewhere for that matter.

The next day they held a meeting, and one of them, their leader in the Warsaw insurrection, gave orders and made decisions, as if there were anything to organize other than the dress, the blanket, the bowl and spoon that belonged to each inmate. But two days later she ordered my sister to be tossed out. "She is like a leper and may infect all of us!" she argued. "And she is dying anyway. We don't want her in here."

Then my aunt and the rest of the girls got organized too. They rose up as one and warned them, "Don't you dare touch her, you dirty swine! You are not in Poland here. You are fat and strong but we are the majority so you'd better be careful. Germans don't come in here unless they need someone for work. Be realistic—here in Bergen-Belsen we are all equal."

That stung. They jumped out of their skins. "How dare you compare yourselves to us," they screamed. "Too bad we don't have a mirror to show you how you look. Look at you—you're not even human anymore. It's frightening just to look at you. And why are you here? Why did they put you in ghettos, kill you, burn you, send you away to do hard labour? Have you got an answer?"—"It's time we knew the answer," whispered one of our girls to another—"But look at us, we are rebels! Our capital, Warsaw, rose up against the Nazi invaders and we helped chase them out of our country. We know why we are here, and if we die, we'll know what we are dying for, for our national honour. But what will you die for? We were caught because Stalin betrayed us. The Red Army was sixty kilometers from Warsaw and did not come to our aid."

"Well," said one of our girls, "at least now you know the taste of betrayal. How did you betray our boys and girls who fought to the last in the Warsaw ghetto? You knew very well that the bunkers were full of Jewish families, without water; that mothers killed their own children to end their suffering; that one killed the other, having no way out. Yet you stood and watched

complacently as if they were burning out fleas and did not raise a finger to help. And when the Jewish underground in the ghetto in Warsaw offered co-operation to your leaders, you rejected it."

"Of course we rejected it," their leader said. "Our struggle and yours was different."

"What do you mean, different? Don't we have the same enemy?"

"Yes, but the Germans destroyed you for racial reasons, while we fought as patriots against the invader occupying our country. The aim of our underground was to liberate our country and win a free Poland once again."

I looked at our girls. They stood, white, filled with tension and anger, and for a long moment no words would come. Then one spoke. "At least here, in Bergen-Belsen, you could find the grace to speak a lie, even if you can't feel it. You couldn't fight with us. You say we are destroyed because of our race, and you are patriotic fighters. At least we know that you are racists too—like Hitler. So you think we are inferior. It's a pity that the millions of Jews and free-minded people still alive in the world cannot hear you, for you'd turn them all into devoted Zionists. All of us were born in Poland. Our fathers and forefathers built Poland. We contributed to every field in Poland's economic and cultural life for centuries. And now you have the audacity to tell us there was no room for co-operation between the Polish and Jewish undergrounds because of Hitler's mad theories of racial supremacy."

"This would be funny if it were not so sad," remarked another of our very intelligent girls. "You consider yourselves superior

to us. How many Poles contributed to the world? We can count them on one hand: Chopin, Marie Sklodowska, Copernicus, Mieckiewicz—okay, we'll give you another one, you have five. And the Jews—Marx, Einstein, Freud, Jesus—these men changed the world. And then there are all the writers, scientists, musicians . . . the list is so long you can't name them all. You forget that Jerusalem and Athens were the source of European civilization when Poland was still a barbaric wilderness. We could call ourselves superior for all the contributions the Jews have made to mankind. But we believe that all people are equal in their human rights and that there are no superior or inferior nations. Certainly here we are all equal."

The Polish girls tried a different tack. One of them spoke out, "As a matter of fact, I cannot see how you expect us to cooperate with you when your own people help in your extermination. We know your brothers took victims from the gas chambers to the crematoria."

At that moment one of our girls, trembling with rage, threw herself forward from the other end of the barracks.

"Silence!" she shouted. "Listen carefully, girls. We are on the brink of death, but if one of us will enjoy one day of freedom, let her tell my words to the whole world. Let the world know that I built Auschwitz and I lived in the shadow of the smoke coming from the furnaces burning day and night for four years. Those who accuse us of complicity will be people like you, people whose consciences are not clean and want to hurt the Jewish soul. Those who did not live it do not know the truth."

"And this is the truth. The first transport that arrived from Poland preferred death rather than help in the extermination of their brothers, and they went to the gas chambers of their *own free will when the Nazis wanted to compel them to take part in the extermination process. Next the Nazis selected Jews from France, Greece, Holland and other countries, and they too preferred death. When the Germans saw that the Jews would rather die than do this job, they set up an example that no human being could withstand. They did not let them die of their own free will—no, they took a group of ten prisoners in reprisal, put them in a cellar, starved them, and made them die slowly of hunger and thirst. A priest, Father Kolbe—a very honourable man—died that way. He volunteered to replace a younger man, an army sergeant who had a family. It took him fourteen days to die. It was terrible to see. The cries and screams of those people set an agonizing example. If the Jews did not obey, the Germans would only torture another group, and another one. The Jews knew very well they were not saving their own skins, for every three months the Nazis exterminated one unit and replaced it with another. Believe me, these people would have preferred to die rather than see their own wives, mothers and children gassed and burned to death. We should remember them with great pity, for all the terrible suffering they went through before being killed themselves. There is no ground for accusations against them."*

When she finished, we addressed the Polish girls from Warsaw almost in a chorus: "We warn you, don't touch this little girl. She is not a leper. For six years she has had to fight for her life. The real danger for all of us is immediate. Look out the window—all those who are being burned now were human beings like the rest of us. Despite our differences in opinion, we need each other and this is the only way to hold on."

For a few days the tension continued. We took turns standing guard beside my sister. Whenever any of them approached they would hear the same words: "We may be thin and weak, but as *long as we live this girl will not be thrown out of the room among the dead!"*

The Polish girls held another meeting and as I watched I knew they were scheming against her. But nothing came of it, for we kept guard all the time. Nevertheless my sister was in great danger and her condition was growing steadily worse. Every morning I looked to see whether she was still breathing. Then one morning we heard a shout, "Achtung!"

We jumped to attention as some SS women entered our block. There was complete silence. The head of our block called for volunteers to pick potatoes in the fields. My aunt whispered for me to go as she was too weak, and a few potatoes would help my sister gain strength. I stepped forward. They took a few from each barrack and lined us up in fives. We could barely stand.

There were four SS women and two men. We were marched for half an hour to an open field, but we saw no potatoes. They forced us to run quickly while the women stood at a distance and shot at us. Hearing the shots and lacking the strength to run any further, I dropped to the ground and lay still. Looking around I saw one girl after another get hit and fall. This lasted about ten minutes. I lay motionless, pretending I was dead. When the shooting ceased and the girls who had not been hit began to walk in another direction, I got up and ran up to them. We stood in line and I heard snatches of the Nazis' conversation, punctuated by sadistic laughter. From this I learned that they had taken us out for sport. These women loved hunting, and we served as targets in today's hunt! They were competing to see who could hit the most moving targets and kill them.

We were led to the potato field and made to carry the heavy sacks of potatoes, for the Nazis' kitchen, not the prisoners'. I hid four potatoes in my clothes, trembling lest they find them. Two hard slaps would have sufficed to finish me off. I was about to throw them away but refrained.

After a ten-minute march we were stopped and the SS women began to search us. "Anyone hiding potatoes will pay dearly," they warned. Out of fear I neither threw them away nor gave them up. By pure luck I was not searched and thus was able to bring the treasure to my aunt. We boiled one potato a day and fed it to my sister.

A few days later I saw the Nazi women again approaching our barrack. "No!" I shouted to my aunt. "I won't die like an animal for those sadistic hunters! I'd rather die of hunger." "What are you talking about?" my aunt asked. Only then did I tell her what had occurred in the potato field. But here they were, and I had to hide. Where? I crept out the door and lay down beside the dead bodies there—I looked like one of them anyway. I lay motionless until they picked some girls and went away. Then I got up. Two of the Polish women happened to look out the window at that moment. "Jesus Christ! Holy Mother!" they crossed themselves in fright, sure that someone had been resurrected from the dead. I ignored their exclamations and hurried to the corner where my sister lay to see how she felt after eating the potatoes.

Auntie too was sick, as were most of the Polish girls. After twelve days in the camp the typhus had got them also. They had high temperatures, and lay down one after the other. Their behaviour had won them few friends, but when we saw how sick they were, we forgot all our differences and all the unpleasantness and tried to help. Those of us still on our feet approached them and asked how they felt, if we could do anything for them. Every one of them asked for water; so we formed a line to bring them water to slake the feverish thirst. In their eyes we could read their gratitude. I too forgot how they had wanted to destroy my sister, and for three days I kept on carrying water to them. If ever anyone blessed another, these girls blessed us for the water in their time of need. Try as we did, all this did not help much, and most of them died. The dread disease mowed down healthy and sick alike, strong and weak, young and old.

Now my aunt needed attention. For a few days she had complained of feeling sick; this particular night she fell asleep and later awoke, asking me to give her some orange juice from the cupboard. What? Orange juice! But when I put my hand on her forehead, it was burning hot. In her ravings she would ask for all the good drinks of the old days. I brought her water, which seemed to be an acceptable exchange. She would babble about dances and parties, picturing herself at a table laid with the finest linen and laden with such foods as we had not seen for five years. I did not know how to help her but finally took off my blouse and, soaking it in water, kept putting it on her hot head as a compress. She felt easier and fell asleep for a few hours, but then awoke, this time seeing herself in a concert hall and demanding her beautiful black dress. In the morning some girls who had been with us all these months, and knew Auntie well, advised me to take her to the "sick block"; maybe she would feel better there. Two of them supported her under the arms, and thus we managed to get her there.

It was April, planes were flying overhead, dropping leaflets with the message, "We'll liberate you soon. Hold on!" A few days later my sister stood up. I could not believe my eyes. She insisted on going to the sick block to see my aunt. "Please don't stay long. I feel terrible," I told her. When she returned, she brought news that the Germans thought the arrival of the British was imminent. They were shooting recklessly, and many prisoners had lost their lives. My sister, too, was shot at but was miraculously unhurt. As she told me about it, I just managed to tell her not to leave again, that it was too risky, when a frightful chill shook my whole body. As I was pulling the blanket around me, I lost consciousness.

When the British liberated the camp a few days later, I was unconscious and in a bad way, but still breathing. My aunt meanwhile had improved; her temperature was down to normal. Slipping out of the sick block unnoticed, she somehow crept weakly back to our barrack and found me in critical condition. She leaned down, called to me, begged me to open my eyes and wake up. She could not believe that I would die now that freedom had come. Finally I opened my eyes, but only for a second. Many were sure I was done for. But they took care of me, and whenever I asked for a drink, fed me hot sweet tea. After three days of this, I regained consciousness and at once wondered where the tea was coming from. When I was finally able to ask, they told me we were free. "Free? FREE? Do you feel all right?" was my unbelieving reaction. Now my health began to improve, and I started to eat. It took a whole week for me to realize that we were indeed free. The dream of five years had come true. I looked at the British soldiers but kept asking whether we could talk to them—were there no Germans in the camp?

When told a shower was available in the camp, I could not believe it until I'd had one myself and exchanged my lice-infested clothes for fresh clean ones. What a heavenly feeling! Immediately I felt like a different person. Old forgotten feelings of shame and pride came forward. Our sensitivity re-

turned to us, we again became shy, asked for a comb and looked after ourselves. We stopped being prisoners and became aware once more of the sensations and needs of normal human beings. New perspectives opened up before us. Although I was not yet up to making real plans, the first thing I wanted to do was to leave this place. Even this was granted me: near Bergen-Belsen was a German army camp from which the Germans had been driven away, and it was now available to us. Before moving in there we underwent a thorough disinfection. We took a hot shower and then passed naked into a hall where young British soldiers sprayed us with white disinfectant from machines. My sister and I were still under-developed for our age, not even adolescents—but some of the women covered their faces with their hands and, though this treatment was vital and essential, it somehow humiliated them and they felt bitter about it. Next we entered a hall where we were given clean clothes, then driven by car to Graben and assigned various rooms there.

Opening the window there was like entering a new world, a world in which we were free, had rights and demands, with no fear of having to serve as targets in a hunt, a world without shouts in the night and permanent hunger. How different were the nights in our new residence! Every morning I woke from terrible dreams to find again that it was all behind me, that I had been born anew. Tortured by repeated nightmares, I began to avoid going to bed and would instead sit looking out the window facing the main street. I liked to watch girls walking with soldiers in complete abandon, as if the years of imprisonment made everything permissible. The soldiers would call out to the girls, "Chocolate? Promenade?" Some merely laughed and walked on, but others accepted the offer with all that it implied. A bar of chocolate sufficed to start a flirtation with a girl who for years had not tasted sweets. As their physical con-

dition improved, more liberties were taken. I watched, and I laughed.

As for me, I spent the first weeks sleeping and eating. Going to bed late to avoid the dreams, I would ask not to be wakened until I was ready. I also ate till I could eat no more. When at last I'd had enough sleep and food, I began to think and take stock of my position. "Who and what am I? What can I make of myself? Have I lost everything, and is it too late to begin anew?"

And I came to the conclusion that, no, it was not too late, in spite of the loss of six years when I should have been studying and enjoying my youth, my home and family and all those relationships that growing youngsters normally have. A wave of despair swept over me again—I felt miserable, such a lightweight, a big zero. "Could I become a normal person now that I was free? Who would guide me and encourage me, with my mother dead and my father vanished, all my dear ones either gone or no better off than myself?" The other girls, being older, had a definite goal—marriage and a family. You could see that all around in the natural way they entered into flirtations and romances. But this was not for me. I was too young, too innocent and ignorant of what it meant. The word sex did not mean a thing to me. Even biologically I was not yet a woman. There was no one close to me with whom I could discuss these matters candidly, so I had to rely on myself. My conclusion was that I was too young for love and must first acquire some education and independence. While I was mulling this over, there was a sudden knock. In came a good-looking young man. Greeting me courteously, he asked, "Does Mrs. Frischer live here?" He had come to inquire of my aunt about his sister, learning that we had all been together for months. His question distressed me; I did not want to be the one to tell him she had contracted typhus and died just before liberation. So I hedged, saying, "Oh, yes, I knew her very well; she was a lovely girl. We were together for a long time but our paths parted in Bergen-Belsen. Someone else may be able to tell you more."

"Maybe your aunt?"

"No, she only knows what I do because she was with my sister and me all the time. You'd better ask some of the others. Many knew her.'

"I've been looking for weeks," he told me. "I've got to find her, or news of her, whether she is still alive . . . ."

When he left to talk to the others, he said he might come again to speak to my aunt; but he did not come back. Someone had told him the heartbreaking news. A few days later another young man came knocking at our door. He asked similar questions of my sister and me. But this time we both cried, "Yes, yes, we know her, she is alive and well. We were together all this time, and we used to help one another. She is in one of these rooms, just go and look and you're sure to find her. She told us so much about you. To find a brother or sister these days is real happiness!"

"You're right," he agreed. "She must know right away that she is not alone!" And he hurried out.

Everyone was searching for relatives. The survivors now wandered from place to place to find any relative, near or distant, anyone to call their own, so as not to be all alone in the world. They dreamed about it in their sleep and, when awake, looked up hopefully every time there was a knock at the door. Many *did find members of their family, and we still had some hope we might yet see our father, cousins, aunt. But where, how? We were in no condition to travel and had therefore to stay where we were for the time being. But it made us happy to learn that our names had been sent off as part of a list of survivors to all the main centres in Poland. They would be able to find us, we consoled ourselves.*

Chapter Thirty

I continued to ponder my future. Again and again the same questions gnawed at my heart: "Who am I? What am I? A little speck nobody notices. I must break through to my own powers, but there is nobody I can turn to, to guide me and instruct me." Many of my thoughts deeply depressed me. I had the feeling we were an unwanted people. We were a bitter reminder to those who had hurt us and to those who hadn't helped us. They didn't want us around.

In the midst of this search through the chaos of my thoughts, I was called to appear with my sister for a medical examination, arranged for all of us under eighteen. My sister was given a thorough going over and told she had to go to the hospital for treatments. I too underwent a thorough examination but did not have to be hospitalized. I did have to be watched and given foods rich in protein and vitamins. Eighty per cent of the girls had to be hospitalized. The medical delegation organized a children's home, part of which served as the hospital and another wing housed the girls who were under observation. They provided an excellent diet, as well as medication and vitamin pills. Now at last I felt that people were interested in us, that they cared and were concerned, and this was warmly comforting.

One person there was particularly attentive and devoted to us. He was Haim, a soldier from the Jewish Brigade, who spoke many languages, a fact of some importance as we were an in-

ternational group. We were very touched when we saw the Star of David on his cap. He used to gather us together and tell us about Palestine. At the end he would always ask for questions. One day I asked, "How much longer will we have to stay in the shadow of the Jewish tragedy? When are we going to be able to leave this cursed Germany and forget the past?"

After a moment's thought he answered, "At present most of you are sick and in need of medical treatment, and the rest of you also need special attention and the good conditions here so that you may regain your health. But plans are being made, and I hope you will be able to leave soon."

One evening a woman came, bringing a girl of twelve who seemed quite nervous and agitated. "I am Mrs. Weinman," she introduced herself, "and this is my niece, my sister's child, Stella." She talked with Haim for a while privately and then left, leaving Stella with us. We tried to be friendly, but when we asked her name, she did not reply. She refused to talk altogether, just sitting there in miserable silence. When called to supper, she did not go to the table, but to a corner where she knelt down, crossed herself, and began to pray. The regular prayers completed, she added a personal one, and we heard her say, "Lord Jesus, and Holy Mary, help me get away from these dirty Jews. I hate them—they crucified you. I'm a good and faithful Christian, and I want only to go back to the nunnery and serve you; but a woman came and said she was my mother's sister and took me away." She crossed herself again, rose and went to the table for supper. We looked at each other but did not say a word. In the morning she knelt to pray again, repeating her words of the previous evening. She did this twice daily.

A few days later, when Haim gathered us all together as was

his habit, he said, "Children, dearest treasure of the Jewish people, when I see how few of you remain out of the millions of children who lived before the war, I want to weep day and night without pause. And my heart does weep within me to see the surviving remnant so sick and so disturbed. I know that each of you has a raw wound in your heart that may never heal completely. But you are the symbol and hope of our people's future. You are our aspiration to fight for our people's independence and security and for a better future for us all, and no nation will ever succeed in destroying us." His words stirred me, penetrating my innermost soul. Then he added, "You are not children any more, for you have the understanding of adults. I ask you to try to understand Stella. Try to get through to her, show her attention and affection, for she is the personification of the second tragedy we have suffered, the aftermath of the holocaust. When she finally realizes the truth, it will be a great shock to her, and she will want to keep it to herself because of the shame she will feel. She will need your compassion. You can help her by being kind. It doesn't matter how many times she repeats this prayer of hers, remember it is not Stella who is to blame. The wrongdoing is not hers. The blame lies with the nunnery she was taken to for teaching hatred and intolerance. Those people forgot the true principles that Christ taught—love, understanding, tolerance, mutual help in time of need. Now some of the monasteries and nunneries didn't do that. Some took in Jewish children, cared for them and have returned them to us; others tried to convert them." As he spoke I recalled the refusal of these institutions in my part of Poland to help us or to conceal the children of desperate Jewish mothers. I didn't know about the others, but judging from the tone and content of Stella's prayer, her benefactors had a lot to learn about the true meaning of religion . . . .

At the end of a week or so, Haim took Stella aside and, seating her in front of him, said kindly, "Listen to me, dear. During the Nazi rule the Jews were all either killed or imprisoned; but now that is over and we are free. Every one of us is free to choose what he wants to believe and what he wants to do in the future. There are nunneries everywhere. If you decide that that is what you wish, no one will prevent you from entering one and devoting your life to it. All I ask is that you think it over carefully and come to a decision that is really your own. We won't impose our will on you, but we don't want to see anyone else's will imposed on you either—you understand that, don't you? To make this decision of your own free will rather than submit to the will of others, you need to know your own origins. You need to find out what happened to your parents and your family. Think it over, and if at the end of a year you still want to go into a nunnery as your way of life, we will not stand in your way. We are free and that means you are free. Now I want to ask you some questions. Where are your mother and father?"

"I don't know."

"But you do know that every child has parents and that you had parents too, don't you?"

"Yes."

"Do you remember them at all?"

"Very vaguely."

"Well, this proves you had parents—but don't remember what happened to them. I'll tell you what happened. The Nazis killed them. And I'll tell you why. Your parents weren't criminals, they did nothing wrong or against the law. They were just Jews, *and you are their daughter. You are alive because they loved you so much that they found a way to hide you from the Nazis—they placed you in the keeping of the nuns they knew, to save your life, not to make a nun of you. Mrs. Weinman is your mother's sister. Here, look at this family picture she left with me—is that you?"*

Stella looked at it. "Yes," she whispered, bewildered, her eyes big and full of dismay.

"Good," Haim smiled, taking the photograph back. "Now remember we love you very much and you are very dear to us, as are all these children who were left over."

Haim devoted a good deal of time to Stella and we all tried to help. She did not go back to the nunnery.

The negotiations regarding our leaving Germany, to which Haim had alluded, were fruitful. We were told that anyone interested could sign up to go to Sweden. The offer was being extended first to the sick and to the young people up to the age of eighteen; they were to be accompanied by any of their relatives. Sweden had volunteered to give us all the help we needed, to bring us back to health, to offer us security and faith in ourselves. They wanted to show us that another world still existed where people behaved humanely, to provide us with the economic and spiritual aid we now required, and with education. In brief, they were eager to start us on a new, normal, productive life.

Sweden! I knew nothing about this country, its geographic location, its history, people or culture. But I did not doubt that we would be among the first to sign up. We wanted to leave the horrid past behind us, the biggest graveyard in the whole world. And indeed we were among the first to board the train for Lubeck, the famous harbour.

When we reached Lubeck, we were brought into a large bathhouse, then into a Turkish bath, and finally disinfected thoroughly. New clothes were given us and then we were put up comfortably for the night in yet another building. From the window in our room we could see the port, ships arriving and departing. I watched them, fascinated, wondering. Were we actually going to sail aboard one of these ships to a country none of us knew? I could hardly wait to get acquainted with the Swedish people, to see how they would receive us. Would they be able to understand us? How would we communicate, since we did not know a word of their language? They would probably find us strange, and we would need to explain our experiences. But how? My worries and apprehensions subsided once we were on board ship, for the warmly devoted attention of the nurses and the entire staff put us at our ease. I enjoyed the voyage immensely except at night, when nightmares brought the past back vividly and I would wake up too terrified to breathe until I realized where I was. I decided not to go to bed anymore, to stay up until dawn. Why should I spoil this wonderful trip with those nightmares?

I stepped from the cabin up to the deck and looked at the moon and the stars and the deep blue sea all around me. I could see nothing but sky and water. It was like something I had never seen, or could only vaguely remember feeling, the beauty of this quiet, romantic night. I walked along the deck for a very long time until a nurse found out I was missing and caught up with me. She asked me what the matter was and I tried to tell her, but she did not understand German. Instead she took me to my bunk and made sure I undressed and went to bed.

In the morning she reported my behaviour to her superior because it worried her. The doctor called me to him and asked me kindly, "Why were you walking on deck when you were supposed to be sleeping? Were you hungry? Would you like a drink of milk before going to sleep?"

"No," I said. "I feel very well and I don't want anything."

"Are the nurses nice?" he probed further.

"Yes, they are very nice," I said.

"So, what is the reason?"

"I am very grateful to all of you, but since my liberation I dream every night about my past. I see myself running and running; the SS chase me and I run in terror, they catch me and shove me into a cattle-car jammed with people, they beat me and threaten to kill me. So I prefer not to go to bed. I am in a beautiful boat and the blue sea and the stars make me feel better just looking at them. Why should I struggle with SS men all night?"

He sat listening, very quiet, very sad. "Now I understand," he said, "but, you know, everybody needs eight hours sleep a night. Tell me, when you fall asleep at dawn, don't you dream then?"

"Yes, I do, but they wake me up in three hours and it cuts the dreams off." Then I begged him for some medicine that would stop the nightmares.

"I wish I knew of any such medicine to help you, my dear," he replied. "You will have to try and help yourself to get over

this. There is no medicine for it."

"How long will it take?"

"I cannot tell. Try to direct your thoughts to the good things that await you in my country. The Swedes are truly a wonderful people. I'm sure that living among us will drive the bad dreams away."

I soon found that he was right.

A few days later we reached Molmo. The nurses called to us, "Come, quick, look at our country!" This city, they explained, was their third largest and an important port. We began to disembark and were received by a big WELCOME TO SWEDEN sign. Greeted by everyone with warm cries of "Welcome!" we entered Sweden in a happy mood and lifted spirits. Again we were led to a bath-house. It was clean and shining, but what puzzled us was the sight of men walking about in the shower-rooms. Every time we started to undress, a man or a boy would walk in or pass by. Blushing, we would stop and wait for him to leave. We were puzzled, too, by the sight of women walking at will through the men's shower-rooms. We were all girls with firm orthodox upbringing behind us and this was, to us, an extraordinary situation. Men coming into the shower-room to wash your back! The next man who came in we tried to tell, in sign language, to leave, but he only stared uncomprehendingly. Finally a young man approached and asked in German whether he could help us. "No," I replied, "we don't need help, but you are in the wrong place. This is a women's shower." He still did not understand for he only laughed and said, jokingly, "I know. I work here. If you drive me away I'll be unemployed."

We appealed to some women who worked there and asked them to tell the boys that unless they left us, we would not undress and wash. The women looked mystified. "Why? They work here just as we do." But the boys, noting our insistence, left of their own accord. We chattered and wondered amongst ourselves. What kind of country is this, we thought. What strange habits! Men who work in showers intended for women! We were indeed curious, and wanted to get to know these people as soon as possible.

When we finished, each of us was given a little bag containing soap, toothbrush and toothpaste, a comb, a mirror, and a packaged hot meal. Buses were waiting for us. We now boarded them and rode for half an hour to a quarantine camp. Here everything had been prepared for us: there was a big, beautiful building surrounded by a lovely garden, with large rooms equipped with beds, cupboards, a table and chairs. It was all spanking clean. A large sign at the gate read WELCOME! We were assigned to our rooms, rested a while after our trip, and then were called to dinner in the dining room. The staff were uniformed. They served us a hot meal. I looked about me in wonder—was it real or a dream?

That night, for the first time, I slept as soundly and sweetly as a baby and awoke fresh and rested. The pleasant atmosphere, the pure air, the fragrance of the flowers in the garden, and the clean bed had the calming effect of a narcotic. The entire staff tried very hard to create a home-like setting for us, and each one remembered to say a kind word to every single girl, remarking on the best trait she had:"How pretty you are","You have lovely eyes", "Your hair is so thick and beautiful". Everybody had something beautiful to say to each one of us. And how we needed it! So utterly opposite from the abuses we had encountered for years, these Swedish people were a healing and timely revelation to us and worked wonders for our rehabilitation. I shall never forget them and will always be grateful to the Swedish crown and people for the marvelous way they restored us to our humanity as well as our health.

After we had been in quarantine for several days, a team of doctors and nurses arrived and began a series of examinations and X-rays. All the ailing were sent to the hospital or sanatorium for specific treatment, while the healthy were granted permission to go out and mix with the Swedish people. I was lucky to be among the latter. Blithely we set out in groups to see what we could see and gather our first impressions of Sweden. On our first expedition we noticed that all the Swedes seemed to be tall and slim, blue-eyed and good-looking. We walked the entire length of a street without seeing anyone with brown eyes and hair. The streets were immaculate and free of beggars. We went into a store. Upon entering, everyone took a number and stood quietly in line. Quiet was a characteristic everywhere, and this same quiet—or serenity—marked their faces, reflecting calm natures and a respect for others. We were excited, constantly pointing out to one another new discoveries. In the evening whole families came out to meet and chat with us, and many invited us to their homes for visits. A good many families also offered to adopt us, not formally but informally, to give us a feeling of belonging, of being wanted and cared for. They sent us packages of candy, took an interest in our problems, and invited us for meals. They sent us holiday greetings, cards, and gifts. They employed every means they could think of to make us happy.

One day two of my friends and I decided to use the first pocket money we received to take a sight-seeing tour by bus. We did not speak Swedish, but we could read the numbers on the buses. Returning, however, we made a mistake. Although the bus we boarded was the number we knew we needed to get us back, there were some words beside the number which we couldn't read and didn't pay attention to. We rode beyond the city line into little villages and at each one the driver stopped for a moment, tossing out parcels of letters and newspapers, and picking up mail. We were so absorbed in watching this that we did not notice we were travelling in the wrong direction. When finally one of the girls saw that the hour was growing late and our stop was not in sight, we asked the driver about it. But he could not speak anything but Swedish. Then a German-speaking passenger came to our assistance and explained to the driver what our problem was. He quieted our worries with a smile: he would be turning around and heading back to town in a moment, he said. Later he stopped, put us on the right bus and told the driver to deliver us to the correct stop. We arrived back late, but happy.

Next came visits to cinemas where, because of our dark hair and eyes, we were the centre of attraction, especially for the boys. They turned their heads to gaze at us and said what evidently were complimentary things about us. We relished their attention.

Toward the end of the week a small group of boys and girls were invited to visit the Eriksen family for Sunday tea. I was among those chosen. We dressed in our best clothes on Sunday afternoon, and the Eriksens came and took us by tram to their home. We entered a tasteful flat, furnished in Scandinavian style, and met two other couples, friends of the Eriksens. Cakes and sweets were laid out on a small table. Some folk music was playing, and the atmosphere was serenely quiet and warm. The Eriksens asked us questions and after each reply they would shake their heads, exclaiming in Swedish, "Incredible! Impossible!" I too had questions I soon asked. First, *about the strange presence of males in the ladies' shower—I hadn't forgotten that. "Is this customary here," I enquired, "or did they think we were not women with self-respect?" Our hostess laughed and then assured me this was customary in their public baths. No one had dreamed of offending us. "I'm awfully sorry," she said, "that you were so hurt, but when you get to know us better you will understand that we Swedes are very free and open in all aspects of our lives. It's quite different from what one sees elsewhere, to be sure, but I've no doubt you will be proud to be part of our people."*

My second question was related to the bus we had ridden by mistake. "Why did the driver toss the letters and newspapers and magazines out into the road, where no one was waiting to receive them?"

"Why," Mrs. Eriksen replied, "they are for the village. After a while the postman comes along to pick them up and distributes them."

"But might not passers-by meanwhile pick up something and no one would even know?"

"Oh, no! This has never happened. Who would take a letter or something that did not belong to him? That would be stealing! I don't think it would enter anyone's mind to do such a thing. We're brought up from earliest childhood to believe in honesty and dignity, and this training has not disappointed us. Was it different where you came from?" Neither she nor her guests could understand why we burst into hysterics at this.

"Yes," we said, "it was quite different...."

When we quieted down, Mrs. Eriksen, a truly lovely woman,

asked whether we had any more questions. So I asked her about something that had become quite puzzling to me. I had noticed, I told her, that while many people who passed the quarantine camp stopped to talk with us, there were some who merely looked at us for a long while in silence. Why was this, I wanted to know. We felt like we were inmates of a zoo.

"Well," she said, "first of all, many people are unable to talk to you because of the language barrier. But I have an idea there is another reason too. Let me just show you something. My husband collects all kinds of unusual things, so we have these clippings at home." She left the room for a moment and returned. "Look at this . . . and this . . . and this." She handed me ugly, horribly repulsive caricatures of Jews, deformed, with huge, hooked noses, that made me recoil in disgust, with captions under them which read, "These are the Jews from Eastern Europe". "These were circulated by the Nazis as part of their anti-Jewish propaganda to quiet any opposition people might have to their treatment of the Jews to convince them they were killing monsters, not people," Mrs. Eriksen explained. "People who were informed and kept abreast of the news knew better than to believe such things. But some people, basically decent people, but ones who had been brought up to believe without question all that they read and heard, and who were absorbed in their own daily worries, tended to accept this propaganda as the truth. They simply didn't know any better. But when they heard of your coming, they went to look at you—and they were probably amazed how unlike these cruel caricatures you are, how good-looking and gentle you are. You can imagine how they must have felt for believing such lies. You understand, many did not want to believe, but the Nazis had a powerful propaganda machine and they used it very cleverly." We nodded our heads . . . yes, we had known it well.

Now I asked whether she knew how many Jews lived in her city. Her guests looked at one another, remarking, "We don't understand." "You know," she said, "the people who go to synagogue as we go to church." And turning back to me, she said, "We don't know, but if you're interested we'll phone the municipality tomorrow and they'll give us the information." This answer made an unforgettable impression on me. I truly felt I had landed on another planet and, in a sense, I suppose I had. I remembered how even as a small child, I was daily reminded of being Jewish.

One of the boys with us asked what Mrs. Eriksen meant by the term "liberal way of life", which she had used to describe Swedish attitudes. She replied, "For a hundred and fifty years our country and our people have not had a war. Our political and spiritual leaders always tried to build our lives on healthy, strong fundamentals: mutual love and understanding, truth, freedom, These are practised all down the line, in every aspect of our personal and national lives, within the family and between the sexes." Much later, when we met unmarried girls who had children and saw how unselfconsciously they were accepted everywhere, we understood Mrs. Eriksen's explanation much better. The children these girls had borne were kept at home, or, if the girl was employed, in day-care centres established for them. It was all so radically different from what we had been brought up to sanction and believe that we did not know how to evaluate it properly. But we went away from this visit with vivid impressions and a great deal of food for thought.

A short time later we were given little folders containing vouchers for purchasing clothes in a number of stores. We were free to choose the store and the clothes we liked for the autumn season. Two friends and I selected a certain address and went out, happy at the opportunity—the first we'd ever had! —to buy the clothes we liked. We had no trouble locating the store, but when the saleswoman addressed us, we found we could not communicate at all. She hurried off to find the proprietor, who could speak German. He looked at us, then asked, "Are you some of the girls who were brought here from Germany?" When we said yes, tears filled his eyes and began to run down his cheeks. "I'm so glad to see you and to have you in my store. You must come to my house. My wife will never forgive me if I let you go without inviting you. I am Jewish too."

"You are Jewish?" we cried.

"Why are you so surprised?" he asked.

"We asked how many Jews lived in this city and the people didn't know."

"How should they know unless they happened to be my personal friends?"

"You're right," we said. And I thought—how true. It is only when people are friends that they find out who prays where. We explained to the proprietor that we could not accept his invitation without getting permission. "Please come to the quarantine camp, and you will be able to get to know many of us." And how did we like Sweden, he wanted to know.

"It is wonderful," we answered enthusiastically. "If all people were like the Swedes, the Nazis would never have succeeded as they did," said my friend.

"Didn't people help?"

"We can't tell you anything about the aid given in other countries, but where we were, although some few risked their lives for us, they were individuals and not the nation as a whole—far from it."

"Did you hear about what the Danish nation did?" he inquired.

"Denmark? No."

"You didn't hear how King Christian and his son Friedrich were the first to go into the street wearing the yellow patch the Nazis had ordered all Jews to wear? It was their way of protesting the edict, and of course all their people followed their example, so the edict had to be cancelled. And then the Danes took part in a secret rescue mission and brought Jews in boats from their country into Sweden."

"This wonderful news never reached us. We were cut off from the rest of the world, but it is so encouraging to know even now."

Calling the saleswoman over, he told her to show us some beautiful clothes, and he promised to come to visit us with his wife.

Another day stands out in my memory. Although so many years have elapsed since December 13, 1945, I still recall vividly that cold winter day when heavy snow was falling and the room was warm and cosy. Early in the morning I woke up at the sound of the door opening. Looking up in the dim light, I was startled to see a ghost-like white form with a crown on her head and a red ribbon at her waist come softly into the room. She was followed by ten other girls in white. All were carrying lighted tapers in their hands and singing "Santa Lucia". Sitting up, rubbing my *eyes in disbelief, I did not know what to make of it. Now I was served coffee and cakes in bed while this angelic group went singing from room to room. At breakfast we were told that Lucia symbolized light and hope, that she came in December when the days are very short in Sweden and it is dark nearly all the time, bringing light and hope into every home. This was a very old tradition—it originated in about 1600. Celebrations were staged in all the cities, with parties in the homes, especially for children, who put on costumes and went from house to house singing and making merry.*

Chapter Thirty-One

Our Swedish benefactors now directed their attention to our education—and set about organizing some kind of consistent program for us. It was quite a school! We all spoke different languages and were all at different levels. At first they simply grouped us according to age, planning to make changes as the teachers came to know their new students' abilities. After a period of experimentation they concluded that the best teachers for us were those who had been sent for this purpose from Palestine. They treated us with the devotion of blood and kin, taught us about our ancestral land and our Jewish history as well as modern Hebrew. Special evenings for informal talks and discussions and for welcoming the Sabbath were also a part of our program, along with Hebrew songs and folk dancing. But perhaps the most significant and effective of all were the teachers' repeated assurances of how especially dear we were to them and to the Jewish people as a whole.

The greatest joy my sister and I had in store for us was the discovery that father was alive. As soon as he was free, although very sick, he made his way back to our town to look for us. Slowly, he recovered his health. When he heard that lists of survivors had arrived, he hurried to inspect them and, seeing our names there, burst into tears. At once he packed a small bag and went in search of us. Going first to Bergen in Germany, he was informed that we were now in Sweden, and he was given permission immediately to join us. I received the news when the headmistress entered our classroom in the midst of a lesson and announced that a cable had just arrived for Chava saying her father was on his way. Not only I but all the others were overjoyed. They all shared our happiness and hoped they too might receive similar news.

I immediately notified my sister, who was still in the hospital. A few weeks later a letter informed me father was in quarantine. My aunt and I hurried over and found him in a large room talking with some other men. We stopped at the door and my aunt said, "You go in first, dear. See if he recognizes you." Twice I walked past him and, although he looked up, he did not know me. It wasn't until my aunt came in too that he suddenly recognized her and realized that I was his daughter. Later, after our joyful reunion, I took him to the hospital where my sister was staying. She was in the garden with some children tossing snowballs at one another. I asked him if he could pick out his daughter among them. He could not recognize her either.

After my visit with father I returned to school. Several months later I was transferred to another school run by a young couple. He was a German Jew who had found refuge in Denmark and married a Danish girl, Inga, who despite her youth, had been active in the rescue of Jews and in transferring them to Sweden. Zvi had been active in the Zionist movement in Germany and had experience with young people and their problems. They worked devotedly and well together and created a warm atmosphere for their young charges. From Inga I learned the full story of how the Danes had saved the Jews who lived in Denmark, and how the Swedes had accepted them into their midst. From these stories, and from my own experiences among the Swedes, I gradually regained my faith in people.

The Danish underground, of which Inga had been a member,

organized the many rescue missions. "First of all," said Inga, "we had our members infiltrate the Gestapo by working for them in all the offices. Thus they were able to get information which they relayed to us. When we learned of their intention to send transports of Jews east, we organized a mission to Sweden. But the Germans got wind of it and were planning to go to the port at night and prevent us from rowing the Jews across to Sweden. We found out, so we organized the kids. We had hundreds of them go there on their bicycles. They formed a barricade with their bikes and held the Germans back when they tried to get to the boats. The kids held them until our boats were in neutral waters, approaching the Swedish shore."

"Another time we learned that the Nazis had a list of Jewish families and were going to arrest them that night. Our people managed to copy the list and we went to everyone on it and warned them. Danish families offered to hide them or to help them get away. Those Jews who did get caught were the ones who did not heed our warning."

We were all sitting, listening open-mouthed. Inga smiled, "You are so impressed with this. We only did our duty as human beings."

"Oh, Inga, you should be proud to belong to such a country. The Jews will remember what you did for a long, long time. It will be recorded in our history books."

When the group had left, I went to Inga and told her, "You'll never know how important it was for me to hear all you told here today. You have restored something essential that I had lost—my trust in human beings."

Chapter Thirty-Two

A year and a half passed in the healing climate of Sweden. I was growing up and felt I ought soon to make a decision about my future. There were two alternatives open to me: one was to remain in Sweden and take advantage of the opportunities offered me to go on with my studies. I knew I was still young and it was not too late. I would very much like to study medicine or a related profession, and the idea of living in Stockholm as a student, something that had fascinated me so long ago, could materialize now. I could live a peaceful life, a life of beauty within a progressive society together with my father and sister. My sister and I were very close; we had been through the Nazi hell together and had never in our lives been separated. "Don't I deserve it," I thought to myself, "after all the horror I've gone through."

The other alternative was to go to Palestine on a so-called illegal boat and help my own people in their struggle for independence. I knew exactly what the circumstances were and what would await me there. It was far from a simple decision. I would have to give up the dream of an education and a profession, and of a quiet, peaceful life. I would have to part from my sister and my father. Many a night I lay awake thinking, not knowing what to do and not daring to make up my mind.

One image kept coming back: I remembered my childhood, remembered looking at my Polish friends cheerfully walking to and from school, while we, my two girl-friends and the Jewish boy, walked alone, afraid of being called dirty names or "*Jew kids, go to Palestine*". All the memories flooded back—standing in the railway station at Sosnowiec looking at the Jews being driven like animals into cattle cars bound for Auschwitz; the faces of the women and children praying only for a quick death; how in Bergen-Belsen I was used for a Nazi shooting target. I remembered, too, how I hated my own people for not securing a haven for future generations and how determined I was that we, the younger generation, must fight for our independence and freedom from fear and discrimination. I heard the man in the ghetto saying, "*If you forgive us it will be easier for us to die*". And the eyes of those children who so wanted to live—and that did it. My decision. If I had lived enough and understood enough to criticize the past, then I could not make the same mistake myself and turn my back on it. If people like me would not go, then the future could again be in jeopardy. I would go to Palestine.

Once I had made the decision I found peace of mind and was able to sleep. Now I faced the difficult task of informing my sister and father of my plans.

The morning I was to tell her, I got up and hung around the room until finally, without preparation, I announced to my sister, "Today I'm going to put the closet in order!"

"You are?" She was surprised. "How come? That's always been my job."

"I have to learn to do it. Soon I'll have to do everything for myself."

"Oh, are you trying to tell me you've decided to go to Pales-

tine?" she guessed.

"Yes."

"Well, Chava, you know how close we are. I've always depended on you. It will be terribly hard to be separated after all we've been through together all these years. But I know you're doing the right thing. I only wish they would take me too."

"You know that's not possible," I gently reminded her. "You're too young and your health wouldn't see you through the hardships. But I promise you that as soon as it is possible, whatever time it takes, I will send two tickets for you and father to come and join me there. Until then, promise you will study hard, and when you come, it will be to a free Jewish land!"

Father had to be told next. "Father, do you think I am old enough to make decisions?"

"Yes, dear, but why do you ask?"

"I've decided to go to Palestine. I want to help in the fight for our freedom!"

"Bless you!" he said fervently.

Finally the day came. I packed my bags and both of them accompanied me to the train. As it came steaming in, I could see my father crying silently. "Don't cry, Father," I tried to console him, "this train is not going to Auschwitz, but to a place which will prevent Auschwitz from ever happening again. You hear me!" And I jumped aboard.

I was scheduled to go on the boat "Exodus" but plans were

changed and there were many delays. Finally I arrived in Palestine with my group on March 3, 1948. Rushed from Haifa to Tel Aviv by armoured car, we heard shots all the way.

Several eventful decades have elapsed since that day. I was not alone in my decision to take an active part in the fight. Many others with a history like mine, or even worse, came to the old-new land to make it free. Some of them had survived all the horrors and dangers in Nazi Europe only to lose their lives in Israel, and our people will remember and be grateful forever to those who died in the struggle. The others, those who lived to see a free and independent Jewish State of Israel established and recognized by the nations of the world, do not as yet know the taste of peace and security. My only prayer is that my own story will help a little to see things as they were; and that such a disaster as the Nazi hell-on-earth will never happen again. We know that in the final analysis we must solve our problems ourselves. This is the great lesson we have learned. We must make sure we fulfill the Will and Testament of the Dead, and remember for all time the heritage of six million martyred dead.